CONTENTS

THE EUROPEAN VOTER:

Popular Responses to the First Community Election

Jay G. Blumler and
Anthony D. Fox

Studies in European Politics 6

ISBN 0 85374-203-0
Published by Policy Studies Institute, 1–2 Castle Lane, London SW1E 5DR
Printed by Bourne Offset Ltd.

Acknowledgements

The authors of this short book owe a large debt to many individuals. The survey findings reported in it formed part of a wider enquiry into the role of broadcasting in the first direct election to the European Parliament, and we wish to record our gratitude to all who made the study possible or assisted us with it.

Credit for initiating the investigation as a whole, and for giving it a London home with administrative amenities, belongs to the International Institute of Communications and especially to its tireless Projects Co-ordinator, Joanna Spicer. More than any other single person - except for our wives - she shared our downs and ups.

The surveys could not have been mounted without the generous financial sponsorship, provided in many cases with remarkably unbureaucratic speed, of numerous sources: the Danish Social Science Research Council, the Directorate-General for Information of the European Commission, the Dutch National Committee for Direct Elections to the European Parliament, the Nuffield Foundation, Radio-televisione Italiana and Westdeutscher Rundfunk. Roger Morgan, Head of the European Centre for Political Studies at the Policy Studies Institute, deserves special mention in this connection for having guaranteed, at a crucial moment, a subsidy should other funds not suffice for our needs. Although in the event we did not have to draw on his offer, without its backing the planned surveys could not have gone ahead. Our thanks are due to him and PSI for publishing the first results of our work in the Institute's series of 'Studies in European Politics'.

We are enormously indebted to all our European colleagues on the project: Giovanni Bechelloni, Frans Bergsma, Kees Brants, Roland Cayrol, Mary Kelly, Walther Kok, Denis McQuail, Gianpietro Mazzolini, Marie-Claire Noel-Aranda, Philip van Praag, Steen Sauerberg, Klaus Schönbach, Winfried Schulz, Karen Siune and Gabriel Thoveron. They shared the painstaking labour of designing a questionnaire that had to be at once comprehensive and economical. They also proffered invaluably severe criticisms of our analyses, interpretations and presentations of the data. Yet we have come to value their comradeship, whenever the opportunity to meet has arisen, even more than their contributions to the preparation of this work.

In pursuing the issues of this study both of us have learned considerably more about European broadcasting, politics and public opinion than we knew at the outset. Our education in such matters was accelerated and enriched by contacts with many congenial representatives of political and broadcasting organisations throughout the European Community, including staff members of the European Commission and the European Parliament. For their encouragement, advice and availability as ever-ready sounding boards, we are most grateful to Roy Pryce, formerly Director of the Directorate-General for Information, and Jacques-Rene Rabier, Special Counsellor, both of the Commission of the European Communities, and to Stephen Wright, Head of Audio-Visual Information of the Directorate-General for Information of the European Parliament.

Much of the analysis was conducted while Tony Fox held a Visiting Fellowship at the SSRC Survey Archive at the University of Essex. Our thanks go to its Director and staff for the impressive facilities that were put at our disposal and especially to the Assistant Director, Eric Roughley, for his help in preparing the data for analysis. Invaluable additional assistance in the organisation of data-processing was given Jay Blumler by Sophie Colleau when in March-May 1980 he was attached as Brittingham Visiting Professor to the School of Journalism and Mass Communications at the University of Wisconsin-Madison. Our approaches to the analysis of the results have also been advanced and sharpened through many discussions with: Denis Davis, Department of Communication, Cleveland State University; Jack M. McLeod, School of Journalism and Mass Communications, University of Wisconsin; and David H. Weaver, School of Journalism, University of Indiana.

Christine Bailey, who is a tower of secretarial strength in the office of the Centre for Television Research at the University of Leeds, typed to the same standards of perfection each and every version of what sometimes must have seemed like a never-ending succession of drafts. She endured this process with more patience and tolerance than we deserved.

Finally, our thanks go to the SOFRES organisation in France, and to the Gallup polling agencies in seven other countries, for carrying out the fieldwork - and to 8,114 interviewees for answering our questions about their experience of the first direct election to the European Parliament.

Jay G. Blumler   Anthony D. Fox

Preface

This book comes just at the right moment: rather less than three years after the European election of 1979 and rather more than two years before that of 1984, and at a time when Pieter Dankert, the new President of the European Parliament, is said to be concerned to improve the public image and the degree of citizen support of that institution. He has a heavy task!

The election by universal and direct suffrage of the representatives of the people of the member states, which was provided for as early as 1951, in the treaty setting up the European Coal and Steel Community, then again in the Rome Treaty of 1957 establishing the European Economic Community, was postponed for a very long time by a sort of mutual agreement between the governments concerned.

At last, in June 1979 - with a delay of only 28 years! - approximately 178 million citizens were given the chance to vote, and of these 62 per cent in fact made use of this right: it was an event without precedent, and one which carried a high symbolic significance, if we ask, for instance, whether the embattled nations of Europe in 1940-45 would ever have believed that they would one day vote together to elect a common representative assembly. And yet, in the end, it was an event which did not make a great mark on the consciousness of the European nations, at least if one judges by the relatively low degree of involvement of the voters, the information media and the organised political forces. It is however necessary to distinguish carefully between the actions and the attitudes of the citizens in question, and again between one country and another, and yet again, inside each country, between one political force and another.

The book by Jay Blumler and Anthony Fox represents a truly original and a most valuable contribution to our understanding of these distinctions - an understanding which is as important for social research as it is for future political action.

In carrying out our own first scholarly research on these elections - at a time when the issues were still very hot - we made an effort to analyse the interacting variables which appeared, in each country and for each major group of the national electorates, to have influenced their propensity to go and vote: the individual pre-disposition of voters ('cognitive mobilisation') and the activities of the news media and the parties ('political mobilisation').(1) However, even though we could already at that time make use of the basic data concerning attitudes and behaviour, thanks to the Eurobarometre surveys undertaken on behalf of the Commission of the European Communities, we were lacking documents, judgements and eye-witness accounts of the actual progress of the election campaign in the different countries, and particularly on the degree to which the headquarters of the major political parties and the managers of the main information media, particularly television, were involved. This gap in our knowledge has now been filled: we now have important new data, and some extremely interesting analyses. Particular attention will be aroused by Chapter V, The Process of Election Involvement, which shows very clearly how the relatively small electoral turnout seems to have been mainly caused, especially in the United Kingdom, by the lack of vigour of an election campaign where the public hardly realised what was at stake, or at least remained very little mobilised by it. It would in fact be unfair, on this point, to criticise the managers of the news media, and particularly of television, the medium which has the greatest impact and the greatest influence on the relatively unpoliticised mass of the electorate. The responsibility for this relatively low electoral turnout in the whole Community, and for the fact that it was really very low indeed in some countries, is a collective responsibility, which falls in the first place on the political leaders, the national governments, the leading organs of the political parties, and the European institutions themselves. Most of these actors, in fact, showed themselves to be more concerned to organise, at the least possible expense, an international ceremony which had now become inevitable than to embark on a European political struggle which might have put forward the idea of reaching concrete, innovative, and publicly exciting objectives.

And now, 'what is to be done?' The next European election will take place in 1984. There is every reason to fear that the same

(1)   See Ronald Inglehart and J-R Rabier, Europe Elects a Parliament: Cognitive Mobilization, Political Mobilization, and Voter Turnout, International Political Science Association, Moscow,   August   1979,   reprinted   in   Government   and Opposition, London, Autumn 1979, and in Contemporary Perspectives on European Integration, Ed. Leon Hurwitz, Greenwood Press, Westport, Conn., 1981.

effects as last time will be produced by the same causes, if indeed things are not worse. At least, no one will again have the excuse that a European election is taking place for the first time.

My grateful thanks go to the authors of this book, which should be read and considered by all who are concerned with the future of Europe, whatever opinion they may have on the European Community as it now exists and as it may go forward.

Jacques-Rene Rabier
Honarary Director-General
Special Adviser for Public Opinion Studies
of the Commission of the European Communities

THE AUTHORS

Professor Jay G. Blumler is Director of the Centre for Television Research at the University of Leeds.

Anthony D. Fox is a freelance political researcher, who was formerly a Senior Research Officer with the British Election Study at the University of Essex and Research Associate at the International Institute of Communications, London.

I APPROACHING THE EUROPEAN VOTER

In June 1979 the citizens of nine Western European countries were able, for the first time, to vote for Members to represent their interests in the Parliament of the European Community. This historic event was unlike any election previously staged in the democratic world. It was the first held to determine the membership of an international deliberative assembly. The European Community, a still politically embryonic body, lacked most of that tissue (in the form of its own party and communication institutions) which normally supports national election campaigns. In addition, due largely to the lack of previous regular mass media attention, few issues had clearly surfaced in advance of the campaign to harness candidates' energies, or to concentrate voters' minds and choices, in the usual way. Even the public service television networks, those great political orchestrators of our age, faced responsibilities in the provision of information, the nature of which was exceptionally difficult to define and the popular response to which was even more difficult to predict. Yet some Europeanists hoped that the very holding of an election campaign would strengthen the processes of public opinion formation at the European level and give the Common Market a much-needed political dynamic. Consequently, the 1979 election was launched in a singular atmosphere, blending faith and scepticism alike.

How, then, did the electors of Europe actually respond to this new call on their attention and participation? Who became involved and who allowed the campaign to pass them by? What information, ideas and incentives to take part (or not) did people acquire through their exposure to the campaign? In what perspectives did those who voted cast their ballots? Were they moved by

1

more European or more national impulses? What part did communication, and especially the dominant medium of television, play in awakening awareness of this election and fashioning its principal outcomes? How did such developments and reactions differ from one European country to another? And how did the first European election shape up as a political occasion overall - in comparison, say, with the usual run of domestic general elections?

Such issues are explored in this study by drawing on evidence from a series of comparative surveys that were carried out shortly after polling day in eight of the nine member states of the European Community.(1) Overall, two broad purposes have guided our use of the resulting data. First, regarding the European election as a peculiarly complex and problematic venture, we have aimed to clarify, by recourse to the testimony of mass publics themselves, its main results, achievements and failures. Second, recognising that the campaigns constituted a uniquely simultaneous occasion of international political activity and message propagation, we have seized the opportunity to compare processes of election communication across a number of different national party and media systems. The background to each of these purposes is outlined in the next two sections of this chapter.

A problematic election

In advance, the first election to the European Parliament awakened both hopes and fears. Enthusiasts had looked forward to it as a historic milestone in the political evolution of the European Community. At last giving the man in the street something to 'do' for Europe, it could perhaps involve him more actively in tasks of European construction (Colombo, 1969). It could strengthen the legitimacy and authority of the European Parliament itself, by enhancing its visibility, intelligibility and relevance in the eyes of European citizens (Pryce, 1976). It could accordingly initiate the democratisation of Community politics, as well as whet the political appetites of the successfully elected MEPs to assert and perhaps even increase the powers of the European Parliament (Steed, 1971).

Those who approached the election with such hopes envisaged it, then, as a promising vehicle of change, popular involvement and Community-building. Despite formidable organisational problems and the drag of mental inertia, it at least offered a chance to lift, or re-direct, the political sights of many Europeans. It might

2

familiarise voters with a different politico-cultural world from that of their national scene, introducing them to its characteristic institutions and problems and situating them among its key forces and options. Yet an emergent political system that was to become more integrated, not over its people's heads but through their very actions and imaginations, would require a suitably supportive communications network. The many speeches, news reports and broadcast programmes generated by the election would therefore have to make advances on several fronts at once: capturing interest; informing people about previously neglected topics; clarifying the voting alternatives; inculcating a spirit of belonging; and extending the horizons of political attention from national to Community boundaries.

All this was a tall order, and even the more optimistic of observers acknowledged that party publicists would experience difficulty in presenting clear policy alternatives to their electorates (Herman and Lodge, 1978). What, then, could bring the campaigns to life? Indeed, if many electors were 'turned off' instead of 'turning out', the enterprise could be discredited rather than legitimated. Even an active campaign might impose strain on the Community's political fabric. The transnational consensus of the old nominated Parliament, built up over a long period, might be shattered by the activation of national differences through campaign rivalry and rhetoric (Marquand, 1979).

In fact, the potential of the first Community election to promote the European cause in popular quarters was problematic on five counts. First, the decision to mount it reflected no noticeable prior demand from the public at large. Its staging was rather a deliberate measure of 'political engineering', instigated in elite circles partly in the hope of generating a greater Community awareness among mass electorates. Admittedly public opinion surveys had 'indicated for years that support for stronger European institutions (was) widespread among the publics of the European Community countries' (Inglehart et al., 1980). But it was unclear whether such a general sentiment, suggesting at best a rather nebulous sensitivity to European affairs (Hedges and Courtenay, 1978; Jowell and Courtenay, 1979), would open many voters' minds to campaign messages and influences. Of course the election, as conceived by its planners, was intended to emphasise the unity of the Common Market, with a single electorate simultaneously choosing the Members of a single Parliament. In other contexts, political scientists and anthropologists have noted the unifying qualities of elections: ostensibly about competition and choice between alternative programmes and candidates, they also generate a consensual affirmation of the polity itself and its rules (Lukes, 1975; Dennis and Chaffee, 1978). This, however, is normally interpreted as a latent function of election rituals. In the first European election, the unifying, consciousness-raising object-ive was to be more overtly to the fore as those hoping to sit in the Parliament strove to mobilise support. But at the level of individual voters, it was always uncertain whether the ensuing campaign would manage to overcome, or would itself be held back by, prevalent popular indifference.

Second, the powers of the European Parliament were weaker and less impressive than those of most national Parliaments. It was chiefly a consultative rather than a legislative body, capable of wielding some sanctions against the main decision-takers but not counting as a decision-taking institution in its own right. Histor-ically, the constraints on its authority had originated in the highly pragmatic form of functionalism attending the birth of the European Community. This included tendencies to put shared economic interests before political unity, to arrive at major decisions through protracted diplomatic exchanges and summit sessions, and to exclude the general public from participation until a fully operational framework had been firmly established. Insofar as the politics of the Community were seen predominantly in terms of national diplomatic and governmental negotiations, it might be difficult to explain why Europeans, particularly those who were sceptical or indifferent from the start, should care who represen-ted them in Strasbourg and Luxembourg. It was possible to argue, of course, that the election would strengthen the Parliament's hand, that democratically elected representatives would be more keen to exploit the channels of influence available to them, or that they would seek to extend their powers vis-a-vis the Council of Ministers and the Commission. But such arguments were likely to highlight the weakness of the Parliament's formal powers and/or to provoke suspicion amongst those anxious to preserve national sovereignty either within or outside the Community structure.(2) Meanwhile, voters' initially hazy perceptions of the European Parliament imposed an unavoidable 'double bind' on would-be providers of explanatory campaign materials. To give some impression of the body in which elected Members would sit, much programme time and many column inches had to be devoted to items about the Parliament. But in thus focusing attention on such a complex institution with such uncertain powers, there was a

4

danger of confusing and alienating portions of the electoral audience.

Third, despite the aspiration to use the election to symbolise the unity of Europe, both the polling rules and the party and media campaigns were organised along nationally distinct lines. The procedures governing voter eligibility, the numbers and boundaries of constituencies, the methods of ballot counting, and even the designation of polling day, were settled differently and separately by each member state largely in accordance with its normal voting practices. Yet by adapting those practices to the dimensions of the European election, a series of hybrid arrangements emerged, which were neither entirely compatible with normal national rules nor a new uniform European pattern (Herman and Hagger, 1980). Similarly, the candidates who canvassed support were put up by the national party organisations of each country. Although Christian Democratic, Liberal and Socialist Federations issued common statements of principle and produced some Community-wide publicity for the occasion, national parties were jealous of their rights and unwilling to concede other than limited functions to such transnational bodies (Claeys and Loeb-Mayer, 1979; Pridham and Pridham, 1981). So far as communication was concerned, it was commonly supposed that broadcasting would have a major part to play in presenting, reporting and explaining the election to its voter-audience members (Steed, 1971; Blumler, 1979). But any such role would necessarily be performed by national broadcasting networks, each taking its own policy decisions about the amount and forms of political party access to the airwaves, the volume of news coverage and the types of informative documentaries and current affairs discussions that would be relayed. Attempts were made through the European Broadcasting Union to enhance broadcaster co-operation during the election and to strengthen the European dimension of reporting. But that effort was almost entirely focused on exchanges of materials for use in networks' programmes on the election results leaving the bulk of the campaign coverage in the hands of the national broadcasting services (Blumler and Petersen, 1981). To become operative, then, the European election had to be domesticated: the new European wine had to be poured into old national bottles. The election was adapted to each country's particular electoral, political and media systems, and what emerged would depend very much on what those national systems injected into it (Blumler and Fox, 1980).

5

Fourth, the campaign commitments of the main bodies that normally mobilise electoral participation - the political parties and mass media organisations - were in some doubt, although their specific uncertainties and individual ways of coping with them varied greatly across the nine Community countries. Again we are to some extent drawn back to the origins of the event. Just as there had been no prior demand from the public for the election, so too the parties had shown few signs of demanding the right to compete for seats in the European Parliament. Some of course had access to the elites which had instituted the election. Many were also willing, and a few were even keen, to do combat in this new European arena. But in several member states the election impinged on the political system like an intrusion, not always welcome, into the ongoing flow of domestic combat - 'a stone thrown into the pool of British politics from outside', as Butler and Marquand (1981) have described its impact on their country. The key to the degree and direction of participation by the parties was therefore the strategic importance of electoral competition at that particular time in their particular national contexts. In general, the prizes to be won in a European election must have seemed modest in comparison with those available in national or regional elections; while the value assigned those prizes would depend on specific political conditions prevailing at that moment. A party's incentive to become involved would also depend on internal organisational factors, its impressions of what rival parties might do and the likely reactions of its own national support base. And in individual cases a variety of concerns - internal splits over Europe, lack of activist interest and awareness, limited funds - all could blunt and diminish party activity. Of course, the election had to be fought in the end, and consequently references to European themes would somehow be aired more or less everywhere. But even such references were ripe for subjugation to national circumstances through 'linkages' forged to currently prevalent domestic rivalries (Leigh, 1975; Hainsworth, 1979).

Similarly, mass media organisations could not be counted on automatically to accord the European election campaign the same saturation coverage that a national general election receives. It would be more vulnerable, especially in the commerical press, to the competing news-value appeals of other running stories. The very standing of the campaigns might crucially depend, then, on how Europe's public service television networks presented them. But even they would be unwilling to pay the election substantially greater attention than would be justified by the levels of involvement expected to obtain in the ranks of their two main clients - the political parties and the general audience. There was a sense, also, in which the two-fold aim of the election - that of electing Members and celebrating Europe - would appeal unevenly to many journalists. Providing voters with information on which to base national choices is a fully accepted part of a political reporter's task during an election campaign. Creating a European awareness, particularly in countries where membership of the Common Market remained controversial, was quite another matter - likely to be embraced by some, ignored by others and resisted by yet others.(3)

Finally, the election was rather untidily embroiled in a tension between its unprecedented character and the appeal of running it along conventional lines. As the first of its kind, it was also a two-edged affair: on the one hand, capable in principle of exciting the imagination and opening up prospects of new communication patterns and political developments; on the other hand, lacking tried supports of its own and creating uncertainty, liable to be tamed by more customary campaign routines and ways of thought. In the ensuing tussle between routinisation and innovation, the former won most of the battles. What Butler and Marquand (1981) have said about the British campaign applies to most other national versions of the European election as well:

few people in the parties or the media had really thought about the nature of a European election. On the whole, they tried to make it like a low-key Westminster election ... most devoted themselves to the customary Westminster rituals.

It is true that by taking over and only slightly adapting long-established domestic campaigning patterns, the parties and the mass media could slip more smoothly into election gear without undue stress and anxiety. But such an approach also ran the risk of extinguishing from the outset whatever sparks of electoral excitement the fashioning of more novel methods might have ignited.

What about the actual outcome? Even after all the votes had been cast and counted, it was still not easy to dub the election a success or failure - or to give reasons for either verdict (Lodge, 1980). The difficulty may be appreciated by consulting Table I.1 which lists, for each Community country, the European turn-out figures alongside those that were recorded at the most recent general election and expresses the former as a percentage of the latter.(4) Of course, level of turn-out was regarded by many observers as the crucial test of the election's achievement, since on it could turn the hoped-for enhancement of the Parliament's legitimacy and its claims for greater powers. Yet as presented in the table the turn-out figures do not really speak for themselves. Their meaning depends rather on what might have been expected of a European election. If general election turn-out was the appropriate norm, then the European results certainly fell short of it in almost every country. From that point of view, we might wish to ask why the European election failed to mobilise a larger number of participants. Yet the casting of ballots by 110 million people in June 1979 was a scale of political activity that cannot be dismissed. And if we take account of all the difficulties involved in staging a rousing European campaign, then instead we might be inclined to ask why, in most countries, upwards of two-thirds of the general election voters were prepared to turn out for Europe as well. (In Chapter V we draw on the post-election survey data in an attempt to explain both sides of this enigmatic turn-out record.)

Comparative analysis of communication processes

The cross-national analysis of political communication systems and behaviours is still in its infancy. Although some descriptive essays have appeared in recent years (Smith, 1979), together with conceptual frameworks designed to facilitate comparative investigation (Nixon, 1965; Seymour-Ure, 1974; Hoyer et al., 1975; Blumler and Gurevitch, 1975; Gurevitch and Blumler, 1977), very few empirical studies have managed to profile similarities and differences in voters' responses to the political communication flows and election campaigns of more than some single society. Most of the bulky literature of electoral behaviour and mass media effects, for example, is based on surveys conducted in individual countries only.

Yet the results of those cross-national enquiries into political communication that have been reported do tend to confirm the value of a comparative approach. This stems from the possibility afforded of distinguishing communication patterns which can be generalised cross-nationally from country-specific ones, the sources of which may be traced to system differences across the societies concerned. For example, Sauerberg and Thomsen (1977) have thrown light on Scandinavian voting behaviour from the 1950s to the 1970s by comparing and contrasting the impact of evolving media systems on party systems (and vice-versa) in Denmark, Norway and Sweden. In a study of the British, French and Belgian

8

elections of 1974, Blumler, Cayrol and Thoveron (1978) found many cross-national similarities in voters' motives for and methods of following their campaigns, as well as differences in the variables that had structured their media expectations and preferences. Demographic factors were chiefly influential in shaping voters' campaign responses in Britain; political affiliations in France; and regional/linguistic divisions in Belgium. More recently, Asp and Miller (1980) have reported a mixed pattern of similarities and differences in media usage for political learning among American and Swedish voters, ascribing some of the charted variations in turn to differences in the educational and party systems of the two societies.

But the European election offered a quite rich and unrivalled scope for cross-national enquiry. It was as if it had unleashed nine communication campaigns, the involvement of electors in which could then be systematically compared on many dimensions. That is why, when presenting the survey evidence in the following chapters, we often look to see how far the several electorates had responded in like manner, while trying to isolate the more deviant national patterns. In addition, we attempt, where possible, to explain the latter by referring to distinctive features of the campaign organisation, communication systems or cultural environments of the countries concerned.

Survey organisation and design

Our evidence about European voters' reactions to the 1979 campaign was collected to form one 'leg' of a broader comparative enquiry, organised by the International Institute of Communications, into the role of broadcasting in the first direct election to the European Parliament. That study was designed by an international team of European political scientists and mass media scholars,(5) who decided from an early stage to examine communication performance in the campaign 'in the round'. This commitment implied that it should be treated as a system of inter-connected elements, including a) its origins in the policies, intentions and attitudes of mass media and political party personnel, b) its actual message features, as reflected in broadcast programmes, as well as c) its corresponding electoral reception and impact. The investigation accordingly focused on three main levels of the election communication process. First, it explored, as inputs to the process, the orientations to the forthcoming campaign of the major political parties and broadcasting organisations. In both cases the principal instrument was a semi-structured interview schedule, by means of which key personnel were asked, in advance of the official campaign, about the European election policies of their organisations, the campaign problems they anticipated and how they might be dealt with, their perceptions of each other's campaign roles and how they might work together, and their impressions of audience members' needs and interests. Second, the project recorded, and coded to an agreed format for analysis, all programme materials broadcast on European Community topics by the television networks of each country a) during the campaign and b) during three selected weeks running up to it in early 1979. Third, it gathered information about the responses to the campaign of the electoral audience. At this level two forms of enquiry were pursued. In three countries (Britain, Germany and the Netherlands), special grants enabled panels of respondents to be interviewed both before and after the campaign in order to measure informational and attitudinal changes over time and the influence of election communication on them. But it was recognised all along that the chance should not be missed to find out how far the national electorates had reacted similarly or differently to this common political event. This called for the design of a comparative survey to be put into the field shortly after polling day, funding for which was obtained from a variety of sources. The questionnaires for this exercise were in most essential respects identically worded for each national survey.

Survey research is costly, and in this case the expenses to be incurred had to be multiplied by the number of countries to be covered. The national research teams associated in the IIC enquiry were therefore constrained to fashion a strategy covering as much ground with as few questions as possible, tapping the most important dimensions of audience response while respecting tight budgetary limits. They were also conscious of the desirability of putting some questions in wordings identical to those adopted in past surveys of European opinion. In the event, they decided to collect evidence in six key areas.

First, to what extent were voters interested and involved in the election? Did they follow the campaign? Did they recognise emergent issues? Did they vote? Did they know the final outcome (who 'won' the election at the European level)?

Second, on which channels did people rely most heavily for election information? In particular, how did television fit into the overall web of interpersonal, mass media and party-originated communication flows?

Third, how was television coverage of the campaign evaluated by viewers for both quantity and quality? Did they think that their TV networks had paid too much or too little attention to the election? Did the programmes clarify and enliven, or were they confusing and dull?

Fourth, did the campaigns generate a focused issue-agenda of which electors were aware? Were the campaign issues more or less common across the Community or specific to each national situation?

Fifth, on what basis did people take voting decisions? What influenced their choices? In their eyes had their ballots been cast on European grounds or for more domestic reasons?

Finally, what, after the campaign, were their impressions of the European Community itself and their views on their own country's membership of it? How did their opinions compare with attitudes recorded in the past (for example, by the so-called Eurobarometre surveys)?(6) How significant a force, in taking decisions that would affect the lives of people like themselves, did they expect the elected Parliament to become in the future? And how did such attitudes influence voters' participation in the election?

These interests had to be accommodated in a 14-item question-naire, the exact wording of which can be found in Appendix A. Fortunately, the constraints on its design were partly eased by devising ways of collecting information about a series of related matters through a single question format - e.g. finding out whether people had followed the campaign through each of ten channels of communication, or whether they agreed with each of ten evaluative statements about the television coverage, etc. More-over, these election-specific data were enriched by the availability of 13 other questions about people's demographic and political backgrounds, which were included in the interview schedules as a matter of course. Overall, the resulting material formed a data set of 59 variables per respondent, out of which certain additional composite indices were also constructed - measuring, for example, the total number of channels of communication through which people had been reached by the campaign, the total number of issues they mentioned as having emerged from it, and the total

11

number of positive and critical statements about its television version they had endorsed.

The survey interviews were all held in the week immediately following the election with approximately 1,000 electors per country. The fieldwork was carried out largely by companies of the European Omnibus organisation, a consortium of public opinion agencies formed specifically to facilitate European-wide cross-national survey analysis, and was co-ordinated by Gallup (Social Surveys) in London. Omnibus surveys offer the most economical form of polling that is available, insofar as clients buy question 'space' in periodic quota-sample surveys and so share between the total cost of the effort. The cross-national co-ordination of our portion of the June 1979 surveys was complex, however, and necessitated a loss of strict comparability at certain points. For one thing, no Omnibus survey was due to take place in Luxembourg during June 1979. Since the cost of specially mounting a survey there would have been prohibitive, Luxembourg had to be excluded from the post-election voter enquiry. For another, in some countries the 14 core questions formed part of the larger election survey. In Belgium, Britain, France, Ireland and the Netherlands, they comprised the only items about the European election in the Omnibus survey of the month concerned. In Denmark and Italy, however, they were added to a number of other questions, which then formed the post-election wave of a set of two surveys designed to measure opinion trends over the campaign period. As a consequence, in Italy some of the post-election questions were modified to achieve equivalence with wordings that had been used in the pre-election questionnaires. Wherever such changes affect our analysis, however, they are detailed at the appropriate point in the text. Finally, in Germany the post-election questions were introduced into the third wave of a panel survey, boosted by replacement respondents (substituting for individuals who had dropped out of previous waves) to become representative of the country's electorate. The German sample, therefore, includes a large number of people (58 per cent) who had been interviewed on two previous occasions.

Approaches to the analysis

Survey data are open to exploration from many perspectives. Before consulting our evidence, therefore, readers may wish to know what issues and interests guided our analysis of the material described in the previous section.

First, and especially, we wanted to gauge, from a variety of angles, the appeal to voters of this unprecedented election. Before any of its hoped-for objectives could be promoted, their notice would have to be engaged. So how interested was the European elector in following the campaign for his support? How extensively did he monitor it in the mass media and through other communication channels? What sense did he make of its issue content? What influences strengthened or weakened his involvement, including his readiness in the end to cast a vote on polling day?

This focus on electoral involvement was tied to many related concerns. For example, what part did people's attitudes to the European Community itself play in directing their participation? It was fair to conclude from previous survey evidence that many Europeans were supportive of the Common Market in principle, without having had to convert their attitudes to support for any tangible policies and personalities (Feld and Wildgen, 1975). How would these general sentiments fare in the heat of an election campaign? Could campaign communication tap and build on them? Or would their hold tend to weaken for lack of organic connection to urgent issues and keenly felt sources of party division? As the campaign proceeded, did many people begin to form a more concrete impression of the issues that the Community as a whole would have to face in the future? If not, did this matter? And what happened to the minorities of varying sizes who opposed Community membership or were indifferent to it? Did they participate in the election or opt out of it? Perhaps a deeper uncertainty about the very feasibility of staging a coherently focused campaign at the European level underlies some of these questions. Given the current limited state of political integration, how far could Europeans find an election contest set in such a framework meaningful - as a theatre of issues and a set of options for political choice?

There were also questions to consider about the reach of the election process. In advance it was recognised that deeper European commitments tended to be confined to cosmopolitan circles, and it was hoped that the election might diffuse a more widespread sense of European citizenship. This accorded with an approach proposed in one European Community document shortly before the campaign (Eurobarometre No. 11, May 1979):

In order to raise the turn-out on 7 and 10 June somewhere near the norm for a national General Election, the best plan would be to demonstrate the significance of every vote for the future of the European venture and get this message across to the sectors of society which are least politically aware.

How far, we ask, was this aim achieved? Which population groups were most receptive and which most resistant to the call of the European campaign?

In addition, there were the main sources of electoral involvement, especially those affecting voters' participation, to be probed. Which Europeans, defined by demographic and other traits, went to the polls in greater numbers and which ones were more inclined to stay at home? Were the sub-groups with higher turnout rates the same throughout the Community or did they differ from country to country? How important was differential turn-out by the usual supporters of the major political parties? Did the vigour and quality of the communication campaign that was mounted in the various countries make a discernible difference to voting rates? And how can we explain the fact that the turn-out shortfall from general election standards was more pronounced in some countries than in others?

A second focus of our work centred on the reception and impact of European campaign communications. Such an analysis is of interest, not only in its own right, but also for the light it might shed on prospective roles for mass media coverage of subsequent Community elections in 1984 and beyond. In the build-up to the 1979 event, much money and effort had been invested in the promotion of campaign messages - by the Information Directorates of the European Parliament and European Commission, by public service broadcasting networks, by working parties of the European Broadcasting Union, by the political parties and other interested agencies. How did voters themselves react to the resulting materials? How did they evaluate them - that is, which features of the campaign did they appreciate and which did they find less satisfactory or even frustrating? And how, if at all, was their voting behaviour affected? Our eight-nation data have enabled us to seek out evidence of campaign effects on two main political outcomes: people's awareness of the election issues; and whether they voted. In advance, two contrary expectations about such 'effects' could have been formed. Viewed in one light, the European election was a novel event, to which old political allegiances, habits and attitudes might not have been particularly relevant. In that case, it could have given some individuals a chance to form new perceptions and preferences, based on the campaign messages they received, instead of being ruled by long-standing ideas. Viewed in another light, however, if the election's involvement appeal was low, communication during it might have passed many people by, leaving them largely unaffected. Yet if any signs of communication impact did appear, then we would like to know the answers to certain other questions. Who were most receptive to the influence of the campaign? And which of its media vehicles were the most potent carriers of its effects?

Third, we wished to gauge whether this election was a truly European affair for many Community citizens and, if so, in what sense. This is not easily measured, and several different criteria could be applied to the assessment. For example, how far did popular participation depend on voters' attitudes to the Community? To what extent did they themselves reckon that they had cast their ballots on European grounds (as distinct from nationally domestic ones)? Were those electors who voted in June 1979 for parties or lists different from those they had supported at the previous general election (insofar as such individuals could be identified) noticeably swayed by European concerns? And was the possibility of conferring a European meaning on the act of voting effectively blocked by the subordination of election arrangements to national party and media systems?

A fourth aim of our analysis sprang from the multiplicity of the forces that played (as we will show) on the behaviour of European voters during this election. Among others, these could have included: people's attitudes to the Common Market; their party preferences; their demographic attributes; and the extent to which they were reached by campaign communications. From the complex interdependence of all these factors has arisen the exciting challenge of trying to 'model' how they impinged on each other and to show how in concert they may have led to certain crucial outcomes of the election. The results of this exercise have enabled us to attach approximate weights to the role of each of the influences that moulded popular involvement in the European election.

A fifth perspective, foreshadowed by earlier remarks in this chapter embraced the cross-national comparability of our data. How far and in what respects was the June 1979 campaign a more or less similar experience for all Community electorates? In what respects did it take distinctive form depending on varying national circumstances? And to what ultimate factors - of political culture, length of Community membership, linkages of sentiment and interest to the Common Market, or differences of campaign organisation and conduct - might any variations of national response be traced?

Finally, the findings presented in this book should pinpoint some benchmarks, in the light of which voters' reactions to this first European election can eventually be compared with its successors. Of course we cannot predict how later campaigns will be fought or how they will be received by their intended audiences. But we hope that by harking back to some of the evidence detailed in the following pages, it may be possible for policy-makers, mass media professionals and political communication scholars to trace trends over time in the political integration and electoral development of the European Community. Meanwhile, we also believe that the findings should be useful to those responsible for planning the next campaign in 1984.

On quantitative comparisons

Surveys of the kind on which this book's analysis centres are usually subject to a number of limitations. No cross-national empirical enquiry can fully reconcile its need for measurably exact categories of equivalence with fidelity to special circumstances peculiar to the individual states under scrutiny. In this study we have tended to favour the former, while drawing the reader's attention in the text to any departure from common question formats. But we recognise that true comparability is not necessarily achieved by the adoption of identical question wordings; respondents' interpretations of the same question may vary somewhat from one country to another. In addition, we were restricted by both the number of questions which we were able to ask and by the timing of the field-work. Although we attempted through a carefully chosen package of questions to span a number of crucial areas of popular response to the first election to the European Parliament, we are conscious ourselves that these barely scratched the surface. Greater depth, through the pursuit of particular responses by supplementary questions, would have been desirable but could have been achieved only at the expense of the range of areas covered. Finally, a single post-election survey is itself a limited tool for detecting the effects of a campaign, which is essentially a dynamic and changing phenomenon. In order even to attempt an assessment of its impact, it was necessary to ask respondents to recall not only past events and activities but also past reactions and states of mind. It would be unrealistic to assume that such recollections were always sharp and precise. Nevertheless, we believe that the main findings of the surveys afford many useful insights into the reception of this election by the European voter on the one hand, and provide many pointers to important sources of variation in his response on the other.

Surveys are sometimes described as providing photographic snapshots of a public's state of mind at a particular moment. Ours, we freely admit, is a little out of focus. At times the images presented by the data are somewhat blurred. Faced with this, there appeared to be two possible approaches to the task of writing this book. Either we could be circumspect with every finding and surround our conclusions with caveats, or we could interpret more freely, knowing that at certain points we might be accused of reading details into our images that would not be clearly evident to every naked eye. We have chosen the latter course, in part because the former threatened to be even more boring to write than to read.

We are aware too that our evidence is highly numerical. The mathematics, however, are usually not so much difficult as sometimes dense, since each finding, each relationship between variables, needs to be replicated for each of the eight surveys. But we do not wish to limit the scope of this book's readership or alarm potential readers by obliging them to wade through many densely packed tables. We have therefore, tried throughout to explain the significance of our numerical results as clearly and, we hope, as interestingly as possible.

NOTES
1. Luxembourg had to be omitted for reasons spelled out on p.12.

2. Such suspicions were aired before and during the campaigns especially in Denmark, France and Britain.

3. Interviews for the enlarged IIC project (see p.9) with over 200 television journalists, who were likely to be involved in campaign programming, disclosed marked differences over the suitability of this goal both within and across the various EEC countries.

4. The British post-election survey was confined to Great Britain; that is to say, no interviews were conducted in Northern Ireland. For consistency we have presented turn-out figures here and elsewhere which adjust the normal turn-out figure for the United Kingdom to exclude voting in Northern Ireland. However, for the record, turn-out in Northern Ireland in June 1979 was 55.7 per cent and in the United Kingdom as a whole 32.7 per cent.

5. The following scholars have been associated with the project:
Great Britain (and central direction)
Professor Jay G. Blumler, Centre for Television Research, University of Leeds; Anthony D. Fox, Research Officer, International Institute of Communications.
Belgium
Professor Gabriel Thoveron, Centre d'Etude des Techniques de Diffusion Collective, Free University of Brussels.
Denmark
Professor Steen Sauerberg and Vibeke Petersen, Institute of Political Studies, University of Copenhagen; Professor Karen Siune, Institute of Political Science, University of Aarhus.
France
Professor Roland Cayrol, Fondation Nationale des Sciences Politiques, Paris.
Germany
Professor Winfried Schulz and Dr. Klaus Schonbach, Institut for Publizistik, University of Mainz.
Ireland
Dr. Mary Kelly, Communications Research Unit, University College Dublin.
Italy
Profesor Giovanni Bechelloni, University of Naples.
Luxembourg
Marie-Claire Noel-Aranda, Centre d'Etude des Techniques de Diffusion Collective, Free University of Brussels.
Netherlands
Professor Denis McQuail and Frans Bergsma, Department of Mass Communications, University of Amsterdam; Dr Kees Brants, Dr Walther Kok and Dr Philip van Praag, Vakgroep Politiek Gedrag, University of Amsterdam.

6. Eurobarometre public opinion polls have been conducted semi-annually on behalf of the Commission of the European Communities since September 1973. An identical set of

questions was put on each occasion to representative samples of the populations aged 15 and over in each Community country.

Table I.1   Comparisons of turn-out in the election for the
European Parliament and previous general elections

Percentages

	Turn-out EP election	Turn-out last general election	Turn-out EP election/turn-out general election
Belgium	91	95	96
Denmark	47	89	54
France	61	83	73
Germany	66	91	73
Great Britain	32	76	43
Ireland	64	77	83
Italy	86	90	96
Luxembourg	89	90	99
Netherlands	58	88	66

Source: Elections '79:   The Results; Voting Figures in the Nine
and Composition of the New Parliament.   Directorate
General for Information and Public Relations, Publications Division, July 1979.

II EUROPEANS ON EUROPE

With what outlook on Community affairs did Europeans approach the impending campaign of May and June 1979? In the previous chapter we raised certain questions about the ability of an unsolicited election to arouse the interest of mass publics. Such prospective indifference was not to be confused with antagonism. On the contrary, the evidence of a Eurobarometre poll in April 1979 pointed to wide support for both the ideal of European unity and the idea of holding parliamentary elections. Three out of four of the Parliament's potential electors, according to the poll, favoured 'efforts being made to unify Western Europe' (ranging from highs of 83 per cent approval in Italy and the Netherlands to lows of 48 per cent and 63 per cent in Denmark and Britain respectively), and overall a similar proportion favoured holding direct elections. To both questions, the bulk of the remainder gave non-committal rather than negative replies. However, it was always uncertain whether these somewhat abstract and passive indications of support could be converted into active participation in an election campaign. On the basis of answers to yet other questions, for example, the authors of the same Eurobarometre report predicted a rather 'low poll' of 65 per cent 'probable voters' throughout the Community as a whole (Eurobarometre No. 11, May 1979).

Individuals' prior attitudes to Europe were clearly important: there was a strong and plausible assumption that favourable dispositions to the European Community should encourage election involvement. But it is not for their influence on individual motivations alone that such attitudes deserve consideration. Similarities and differences in their distribution across national

21

electorates could show how far Europe had become an attitudinally unified Community by 1979 and along what lines it was still divided. Past changes in opinions over time could yield pointers to their likely malleability in campaign conditions. And pervading the overall climate in which the campaigns were fought, the aggregated opinions of individuals in each of the nine political systems could have differentially affected the election strategies of party managers and media publicists. In this chapter we address these possibilities by examining opinion climates in the several member countries from three perspectives. First, we look at the evolution of Europeans' views about the Common Market over a five-year span of time from May 1974 to shortly before the opening of the official election campaign in April 1979. Second, we describe how our own sample members reacted to three questions about Community politics just after polling day. Third, we inspect opinion changes between April and June 1979 for preliminary signs of a net impact of the campaign on overall levels of public support for the Community.

Cross-national trends in Community opinion before the election: 1974-1979

In the past, one of the more sensitive guides to the evolution of popular sentiment towards Europe has been the following Eurobarometre question, which focuses on the national advantages and disadvantages of Community membership:

Generally speaking, do you think that (your country's) membership of the Common Market is a good thing, a bad thing, or neither good nor bad?

The distributions of response to this question, obtained from the eleven Eurobarometre surveys conducted between May 1974 and April 1979, appear as a series of national profiles in Figure II.1. Each column of the profiles depicts the proportion of sample members giving each of three main replies to the question ('good thing', 'bad thing', 'neither good nor bad'), while the gaps between the tops of the columns and the 100 per cent line register the levels of 'don't know' replies plus all other forms of non-response. The figures beneath each nation's profile are average percentages for each response category over all eleven surveys of the entire five-year period.

Displayed in this manner, the data pick out some little-noticed national differences in populations' reactions to the European Community. Published Eurobarometre analyses of such material have usually drawn attention to a fundamental distinction between opinion patterns characterising five of the original member states (Luxembourg is not dealt with here because of its exclusion from our own post-election survey) and those obtaining in the late-comer states (Britain, Denmark and Ireland). The profiles presented in Figure II.1 clearly confirm the existence of such a 'generational' divide. Average levels of support for Community membership in the five original member countries were all higher than those found among the newer entrants. More significantly, the mean percentages for those taking a negative view of membership were considerably lower in the former than the latter group. Yet within each generational 'camp', some significant national differences of response to the question can be discerned as well.

Among the original member states, for example, the Netherlands stands out as having uniquely hosted a clear and consistent increase in public support for the Community since 1974. The number of Dutchmen declaring Market membership to be a 'good thing' rose over the five-year period from 66 per cent to 84 per cent. This development was due almost entirely to a corresponding decline in the number of respondents giving what we would term 'middle-ground' responses. In the 'middle-ground' we include both those saying that membership was 'neither good nor bad' and the 'don't knows' and those not answering at all. Such a portmanteau category clearly spans a wide range of reactions to Community membership, extending from those for whom membership is scarcely visible, through those who are aware of the Community but confused about its consequences, to those who, on the basis of their knowledge, calculate that membership offers both advantages and disadvantages. But as an analytical category they may be regarded as a single body of opinion in that they are unable or unwilling to commit themselves to definitely supportive or hostile positions on Community membership. The erosion of this middle-ground in the Netherlands, then, reflected a growing confidence among the Dutch in the benefits of the Common Market. As a result, they approached the onset of the parliamentary election campaign with the most pro-European outlook of any populace in the Community.

In the four other founder states, opinion change over the five years was marked more by undulating patterns of support than by steady improvement, the fluctuations involved mainly reflecting shifts between those giving favourable evaluations of membership and those offering 'middle-ground' responses. Yet among these countries certain other national differences are also noticeable. For example, whereas the Belgian, French, and (with one exception) German surveys consistently recorded majorities in favour of Community membership, yielding average support levels close to 60 per cent, in Italy the mean support figure was some 12 per cent higher. And although over the entire period, one in three Belgians, Frenchmen and Germans, and one in four Italians, remained unaware or unconvinced of the advantages of their countries' membership of the Community, in two national cases - Germany and Italy - there was evidence of a short-term growth of confidence in the Community (including some erosion of the middle-ground) in the three surveys that were conducted in the twelve months preceding the direct parliamentary elections.

In addition, the French pattern seems unique in one respect. Throughout the period, outright opposition to membership was numerically weak in all original member states. In Belgium, the Netherlands and Italy the opponents never exceeded 6 per cent of those interviewed, and in France and Germany (with a 1976 exception in the latter case) they amounted to no more than 10 per cent. Yet the profiles do suggest that in France the opponents of membership had at least held their ground, and might even have grown after 1976, in comparison with the levels reported from earlier surveys. That record contrasts with the situation in Belgium, the Netherlands, Italy and (to a lesser extent) Germany, where outright opposition to membership showed signs of waning in the later pre-election surveys.

In the new member states, anti-Market sentiment has always been a more prominent feature of the opinion landscape. That said, attitudes to Europe in Ireland are strikingly different from the equivalent British and Danish patterns. From 1974 to 1979 the Irish surveys consistently recorded higher levels of support for Community membership than those registered in the other two countries - together with lower levels of opposition. In addition, despite numerous short-term fluctuations, the Irish outlook on Community membership became ever more favourable over the period charted by the profiles. In fact, the Irish results fall into two stages. From 1974 to the end of 1976 (the first six surveys), a typical level of support was about 50 per cent of those interviewed, with the number of opponents ranging from 20 to 25 per cent of the sample members. Since 1976, the pro-Market majority has increased further, reaching levels more similar to those attained in France and Germany than those found in Britain and Denmark. But opinion movements in Ireland have also been rather irregular, suggesting that Irish reactions to the Common Market were more volatile over the period reviewed than were those of most other electorates.

Opinion distributions on Market membership in Britain and Denmark are unlike those in any other Community country. First, support for membership is much lower. Second, attitudes are more or less enduringly polarised. Thus, in these more sceptical member states, the Common Market has usually received less than half the support recorded in the Dutch and Italian surveys and less than two-thirds of the backing prevalent elsewhere. For the most part, the remaining respondents divide evenly between those who oppose membership and those giving some 'middle-ground' response. Although certain short-term fluctuations appear in both countries' profiles, the overall impression conveyed is one of stability. Throughout the period, approximately one in three respondents felt that Market membership was beneficial for Britain and Denmark, one in three remained unconvinced, and one in three were more decidedly opposed to the Community.

Thus, what emerges most clearly from this review of eight publics' opinion patterns is a rather variegated picture of divergent national responses and levels of commitment to the Community. There is no common European view of the pros and cons of the Common Market and no evidence of a long-term convergence towards one. Instead, the profiles reflect nationally characteristic levels of approval for and opposition to Community membership. Taking three of the more positively disposed states, for example, a 'normal' level of support in Belgium would seem abnormally low for the Netherlands but abnormally high for Ireland. Of course, to refer to 'characteristic' levels implies that stability has been a feature of most electorates' reactions to the Community. And many of the survey-by-survey results do tend to hover fairly closely around their own average national opinion levels - despite the longer-term shifts noted for the Netherlands and Ireland. This becomes yet more evident when margins of sampling error are borne in mind. Nevertheless, some signs of the occurrence of significant short-term opinion shifts do also emerge from the profiles. If views about the European Community are largely stable, they are certainly not rigid. But again these short-term fluctuations appear to reflect specifically national reactions to the Community, in that the incidence, direction, and magnitude of change differ from one country to another over roughly the same periods of time. Since the most publicised political events of the Community are usually conducted and presented like bouts of international diplomacy between representatives of toughly bargaining national govern ments, these differing reactions are not surprising. In such circumstances, popular assessments of member-ship may respond to the perceived successes and failures of governments in defending their respective national interests. The British profile includes a particularly clear example of such a short-term opinion development, stimulated, as it happened, by the membership Referendum of 1975. The strengthening of European attitudes, registered in that year, reflects the political campaign that was waged over the issue of Britain's continued membership and especially the success of pro-Market forces in the Labour Cabinet in persuading sufficient numbers of their colleagues to back a revised agreement with the Community.

Both features of the national profiles may have had some bearing on the conduct and consequences of the first direct election to the European Parliament. Their stability represents the long-term national orientation to the Community, a system-level characteristic that could have permeated the thinking and strategies of campaign planners in each country. This is not to imply a straight-line flow of influence from opinion climate to campaign organisation. The degree of agreement over Community membership obtaining in each state could have a) affected the levels of campaign activity thought appropriate by party leaders and media executives, as well as b) legitimated (or inhibited) deliberate efforts on their part to use the election to promote a more European-minded citizenry. But the extent to which membership itself was a focus of partisan controversy could have mattered as well. A referendum-style campaign could have excited keener interest, though presumably this required the exist-ence of a numerically sizeable sector of opposition opinion and contending parties taking clearly divergent policy positions. More-over, incentives to engage in intensive campaigning might have been somewhat weaker in states where the Community's credit was quite widely accepted, stifling the emergence of party differences and blunting the edge of public debate. Thus, the actual impact of opinion support levels for the Community on election organisation could have depended on how they were reflected in and taken up by the various national party systems.

But the short-term fluctuations of opinion that have occurred in the past were also important, for these constituted people's reactions to political and media messages. A determined mobilising effort, like the one that was launched for the British Referendum, might conceivably swing public opinion in one direction or another. It was, therefore, possible that in May/June 1979 mass publics would respond in some degree to the particular opinion initiatives, consciousness-raising efforts and communication flows that were unleashed by their own national versions of the first Community election.

Community attitudes after the election

How, then, did Europeans feel towards the Community after the campaign was over? Table II.1 shows how in the second week of June 1979 our own eight national samples responded to the following three questions:

Generally speaking, do you think that (your country's) membership of the Common Market is a good thing, a bad thing, or neither good nor bad?

Some people think of the Common Market as being a first step towards a closer union between the member states. Do you think the unification of Europe should be speeded up, slowed down, or continued as at present?

Thinking about the future, how much effect do you think what the European Parliament does will have on people like yourself - a great effect, some effect, not much effect or no effect at all?

The countries are arranged in the table in an order corresponding to the proportion of 'positive' replies given to each question. Again cross-national variety of response is a prominent feature of the results.

Looking first at the overall picture, it can be seen that most electorates were still quite favourably disposed to the European Community and their own country's place in it at the end of the campaign. In six of the eight samples, proportions ranging from a half to three quarters regarded Community membership as a 'good thing' for their country, while a sizeable block of opponents appeared in only two electorates (41 per cent saying that the

Market was a 'bad thing' for Britain and 28 per cent for Denmark). Attitudes to the pace of European unification were rather more varied, but in seven of the eight countries, pluralities said that this should be 'continued as at present', while significant minorities in six samples wanted it to be 'speeded up' and typically only small groups preferred it to be 'slowed down'. The main exceptions to this pattern were Italy (where two out of the sample members opted for more rapid integration), Denmark and Britain (where 37 per cent and 19 per cent of the respondents, respectively, said the process should be slowed down). And when asked how much effect the European Parliament would have in the future on the lives of people like themselves, not many individuals utterly dismissed it - despite its limited powers - as likely to have 'no effect at all' (the numbers responding in these terms ranging from 11 per cent in Denmark to 28 per cent in Italy). On the other hand, few went so far as to predict that the directly elected Parliament would have a 'great effect', and in most countries about half the population assumed that it would have 'not much effect', 'no effect', or did not know what to expect.

Turning to the individual countries, Italy virtually fell into a class of its own, having the most pro-European population on all three counts. Germany also ranked consistently high, and Britain and Denmark consistently low, in European-mindedness of popular reaction to the two more evaluative questions, though not in estimating the likely future effectiveness of the European Parliament. Indeed, the national batting order of response to this last question diverged markedly from those that emerged from answers to the questions about Market membership and European unification. The relatively large number of Britons and Danes expecting the elected Parliament to have at least 'some effect' even suggests that such an impression was more likely to emerge from a campaign that centred on controversy over Community politics per se. In fact, the British and Danish figures partly reflect a tendency for the anti-Marketeers in those countries to say that the Parliament would have a 'great' or 'some' effect on people's lives - presumably an unfortunate one in their eyes. Otherwise, the figures for Ireland again run counter to the thesis of a 'generational' split in European opinion patterns. In June 1979 the Irish electors overall were actually more positively disposed to the Common Market than were their counterparts in the Netherlands, Belgium and France.

Campaign-period changes in support for the Common Market

But did the first European election campaign discernibly influence public opinion in any of the Community countries? Some basis for an assessment is provided in Table II.2, which compares answers to the question about Common Market membership obtained in the April 1979 Eurobarometre with those given by respondents to our own post-election survey.(1) The gap between the two pieces of fieldwork marked the most intensive period of campaigning for the elections, and differences between the two sets of results could arguably be said to represent a net campaign effect on attitudes to Europe.

The figures suggest that the Italian, Irish and Danish campaigns prompted no marked changes in opinion distributions, if allowances are made for shifts between different sorts of 'middle-ground' replies. But in all other Community states there is evidence of some overall shift of opinion during the campaign. The British campaign appears to have reduced the number of 'middle-ground' replies and further polarised opinions - with increases in both support for and opposition to the Community. But in Belgium, France, Germany and the Netherlands, there were signs of some movement away from positive backing for the Community to a 'middle-ground' position. In France and Germany the decline in support amounted to only 6 and 7 per cent respectively, but in Belgium there was a dramatic fall from 65 to 51 per cent of the populace saying that the Common Market was a 'good thing', representing a lower level of endorsement than that recorded in any previous Eurobarometre survey. The Netherlands appears to have experienced the same crisis of confidence to an even more accentuated degree, the proportion of positive supporters of Community membership having plummeted from 84 per cent in April to only 52 per cent in June. From top place in the rank order of pro-European countries in the pre-campaign survey, then, the Netherlands had slipped to fourth place only two months later. To some extent the reactions of Dutch citizens on polling day itself could have played some part in this trend. In comparison with normal national election turn-outs, the Netherland's rate of partic-ipation in the European election was extremely low (58 per cent having voted in contrast to 88 per cent in the 1977 and 83 per cent in the 1972 general elections), and it may be that the attitude figures in the post-election survey reflect in part an adjustment of views to rationalise people's failure to vote. Nevertheless, Belgium displays the same tendency toward greater uncertainty about the benefits of European Community membership at the end of the campaign, though compulsory voting there kept turn-out high. The post-election samples from these two countries were also alike in a) rarely expecting the decisions of the elected Parliament to have much effect on ordinary Europeans' lives and b) including more 'don't knows' on the issue of European unification than any other country produced. The evidence suggests, therefore, that it was the campaign itself which failed to excite Belgian and Dutch electors and cast doubts, temporarily at least, on the advantages of Community membership.

This material lends some support, then, to three conclusions. First, a European election campaign can have consequences for people's attitudes to the Community itself. Second, those consequences need not always be positive; in some cases they may even be counter-productive. Third, an initially high level of public approval could not in itself guarantee the conduct of a 'successful' campaign. In national campaigns, developing characteristic patterns of momentum and direction, other factors were necessary to stimulate movement, and it is to some of these that we now turn.

NOTE

1. It should be noted that Eurobarometre surveys include inter-views with respondents aged fifteen and over, whereas the post-election survey was confined to eligible electors aged eighteen or more. In addition, the Eurobarometre figures for Britain refer to the United Kingdom as a whole, whereas the post-election survey excluded Northern Ireland and therefore refers to Great Britain. However, we do not believe that these minor sampling differences could have a significant impact on the figures compared.

Table II.1   Comparison of national samples' views about the European Community after the election

Percentages

Market membership is:

	Italy	Germany	Ireland	Netherlands	Belgium	France	Denmark	Great Britain
A good thing	75	59	56	52	51	49	38	37
Neither good nor bad	13	34	14	16	25	31	20	15
A bad thing	4	6	16	6	3	9	28	41
Don't know	8	1	14	26	21	10	14	6

Prefer European unification to be:

	Italy	Germany	France	Belgium	Ireland	Netherlands	Great Britain	Denmark
Speeded up	64	42	34	32	29	24	23	7
Continued as at present	11	50	35	35	51	45	42	41
Slowed down	9	7	11	3	12	7	19	37
Don't know	16	1	20	30	8	25	16	16

Expect the Parliament in future to have a:

	Italy	Great Britain	Denmark	Ireland	France	Germany	Netherlands	Belgium
Great/some effect (a)	57 (11)	52 (21)	49 (15)	49 (18)	45 (13)	43 (7)	31 (4)	29 (8)
Not much effect	28	23	23	21	23	35	33	24
No effect at all	(b)	14	11	18	20	21	15	23
Don't know	16	12	16	11	12	1	21	24

(a)   Figure in brackets indicates per cent answering 'great effect'.
(b)   Response category not included.

Table II.2   Evaluation of Community membership: Post-
              election and April 1979 Eurobarometre surveys
              compared

Percentages

	Good thing		Neither good nor bad		Bad thing		Don't know	
	Apr	June	Apr	June	Apr	June	Apr	June
Belgium	65	51	20	25	2	3	13	21
Denmark	37	38	26	20	25	28	12	14
France	56	49	28	31	8	9	8	10
Germany	66	59	20	34	5	6	9	1
UK/GB	33	37	26	15	34	41	7	6
Ireland	54	56	24	14	14	16	8	14
Italy	78	75	14	13	2	4	6	8
Netherlands	84	52	10	16	2	6	4	26

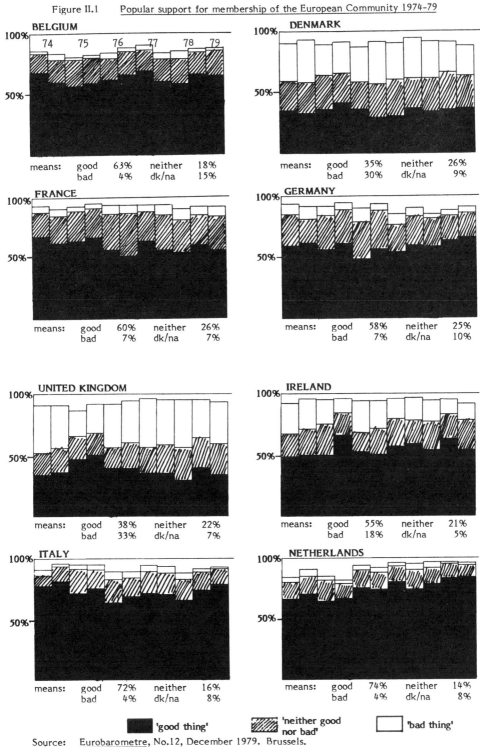

Figure II.1   Popular support for membership of the European Community 1974-79

BELGIUM

DENMARK

means: good   63%   neither   18%
          bad   4%   dk/na   15%

means: good   35%   neither   26%
          bad   30%   dk/na   9%

FRANCE

GERMANY

means: good   60%   neither   26%
          bad   7%   dk/na   7%

means: good   58%   neither   25%
          bad   7%   dk/na   10%

UNITED KINGDOM

IRELAND

means: good   38%   neither   22%
          bad   33%   dk/na   7%

means: good   55%   neither   21%
          bad   18%   dk/na   5%

ITALY

NETHERLANDS

means: good   72%   neither   16%
          bad   4%   dk/na   8%

means: good   74%   neither   14%
          bad   4%   dk/na   8%

'good thing'   'neither good nor bad'   'bad thing'

Source: Eurobarometre, No.12, December 1979. Brussels.

III THE INVOLVEMENT OF VOTERS IN THE CAMPAIGN

In this and the following two chapters we enquire, from a variety of angles, how 'involving' the direct election was for the would-be European voter. We have already pointed out how difficult it was to predict in advance whether Community affairs would matter enough to electors to engage their interest in the contest for parliamentary seats at Strasbourg and Luxembourg. It was also uncertain whether a European campaign would 'come across' as sufficiently significant and attractive to motivate much exposure, learning and participation. Past experience offered little guidance, for individual Europeans had not previously been asked to act in this way. Even in the membership referenda that had been held in earlier years in Britain, Denmark, France and Ireland, voters had in effect taken part in national polls, not an international election. In 1979, then, people were for the first time being invited to assume the role of 'European citizens'. How many would accept that invitation, and how far would the messages of the campaign encourage them to do so?

In this chapter, our approach to this question is based on a country-by-country measurement of overall involvement levels: to what extent did the European election campaign impress the various national publics as an event worthy of notice and participation? In Chapter IV we treat the same publics as if internationally differentiated, and we look at the campaign as a force likely to have uneven reach and appeal to diverse sub-sectors of the potential audience. There we ask which population groups were most and least receptive to the European election. And in Chapter V we treat election involvement, from yet another standpoint, as a cumulative process, fed by a number of sources and impulses, including possibly the effects of exposure to the campaign itself. We ask which features of people's situations and outlook were most closely associated with participation and voting in the election, and how those influences might have worked together to promote or depress electoral mobilisation.

In the pages that immediately follow, however, we are concerned to gauge the overall appeal of the 1979 campaign to community electorates.(1) This focus may in turn be sub-divided into several more specific dimensions of involvement. First, we consider how Europeans reacted to the campaign subjectively - how far it engaged their interest and seemed to them to add up to a satisfying exercise. Second, as a claim on their attention, we next ask how much of the campaign electors managed to follow and through which channels they most often monitored it. More specifically, how important was television as a vehicle for conveying election materials to European viewers? Third, we then regard the election as a potential learning experience, pulling together some evidence on the extent to which people acquired information about certain Community matters in the weeks before polling day and formed impressions of outstanding campaign issues. The chapter concludes with a summary of voters' experience in comparative terms: how similar were the responses of the different electorates to the campaign, and did any national involvement patterns stand out as distinctive when contrasted with the rest?

The subjective dimension: how engaging a campaign?
Campaign interest
    Early in the post-election interview respondents were asked the following question:

> Thinking back to just before the elections for the European Parliament were held, how interested were you in the campaign for those elections - would you say you were very interested, quite interested, only a little interested or not interested in it at all?

Perhaps we should briefly note two features of this line of questioning before turning to the actual replies that it elicited. First, it merges into a single response two sorts of judgement that in principle are separable. For example, a person who said that he was 'little' interested could either have been describing himself as apathetic toward a European campaign or the campaign as an event that had failed to spark his interest. Second, despite such ambiguity, levels of campaign interest could have played a pivotal part in the election process overall. On the one side, they probably reflected a mixture of influences on electors - e.g. their attitudes to the Common Market, amount of past schooling, age, sex, partisan preferences, etc. On the other side, a keener election interest could have sustained or generated a host of other consequences, including readiness to follow the campaign more heavily in the mass media and, as a result, higher rates of exposure to whatever informational, attitudinal and behavioural effects it was capable of inducing.(2)

The eight samples' interest levels are depicted, country by country, in Table III.1. Overall, the evidence suggests that the campaign for the first direct election to the European Parliament was regarded as considerably less than riveting by many Community voters. Across the four offered alternatives, people's responses veered almost everywhere towards a bottom-heavy distribution. Thus, the minority of 'very interested' voters nowhere exceeded 15 per cent. In seven of the eight countries, those who could muster no more than a 'little' interest amounted to between 59 per cent and 71 per cent of the sample members. The difficulties of awakening widespread interest in the European election, then, were by no means confined to the new member states. The indifference of the Belgian electorate, for example, almost exactly matched that of the more determinedly insular British populace. Thus, the more positive attitudes to the Community of the former were not convertible in 1979 into an equally positive approach to the campaign. For Germans, Frenchmen and Danes, however, the drawing power of the campaign, as measured in these terms, was above the Community average. In fact, the German sample's profile of response to this question was diamond rather than pear-shaped, and in Denmark and France nearly two-fifths of the electors were at least 'quite' interested in their campaigns. Seemingly reversing the situation in Belgium, then, the Danish result stands in some contrast to its public's relatively negative view of Community membership.

But is such lukewarm interest all that unusual? Does a national election normally fare much better? We have been unable to locate exactly comparable data from national elections to answer such questions. But in Britain we took advantage of the consecutive scheduling of the two elections in 1979 to tap reactions to both campaigns in another sample of electors, who were interviewed first in the week following the May general election and again immediately after the June European election.(3) The question used in this panel study differed from that employed in the eight-nation survey but nevertheless offers an interesting comparison of response to the two campaigns. Table III.2 shows how the two events were rated by these individuals for interest. The contrast could not have been more dramatic. Fewer than a sixth found the European campaign 'very' or 'fairly' interesting in contrast to just over a half when the general election was being identically assessed. Nearly a half found the European campaign 'not at all interesting' compared to only a quarter responding in like manner to the general election.

Evaluations of the television campaign
    Interest is a summary measure of the popular response to an election. In addition, a campaign's quality can be evaluated on more specific grounds. Did it give people the insights and information they might have expected? Or did it only cause confusion and fail to clarify the available choices? To obtain reactions of this kind, those respondents who recalled having seen on television a programme or news report about Europe in the two or three weeks before polling day were then asked to say whether they agreed with six appreciative and four critical statements about the TV campaign. The top part of Table III.3 shows how many viewers in each sample found at least something positive or negative to acknowledge about the European campaign when judged in this way. And the bottom portion of the table shows, country by country, how often each individual statement was endorsed, separating the positive from the negative evaluations and presenting them in an approximate order of acceptance.

    Apparently, the typical viewer was more conscious of the shortcomings of the European campaign, as presented on television, than of its virtues. In five of seven countries (the exceptions being Germany and Ireland) more respondents endorsed at least one critical statement about the campaign than agreed with some favourable one. The preponderance of negative reaction is further underlined when it is realised, first, that the question offered more positive than negative statements to consider, and second, that these judgements were passed only by those individuals who were already sufficiently involved in the election to have followed it at least minimally on television.(4)

    Thus, the most widely accepted verdicts on the TV campaign were that:

It all seemed rather boring.

It didn't tell me about the advantages and disadvantages for (the country concerned) of being in the European Community.

It left me feeling rather confused.

It is true that the campaign also helped quite a few viewers 'to think more about the future of Europe' and showed them where their own party stood on European questions. But it is also noticeable that few electors considered that they had been helped to 'make up my mind how to vote', even though the European election arguably could have presented new frameworks and posed new issues for voting decisions.(5)

Some intriguing national differences also emerge from these figures. In overall assessment, the German and Irish TV campaigns evoked the most positive responses, while the Belgian and French campaigns fared little better than the British one in provoking more complaint that appreciation. Compared with the other electorates, Dutchmen passed fewer judgements of any kind on the quality of their campaign.

There are even some signs that the policy decisions for election coverage taken by broadcasting organisations had made a difference to viewers' reactions. For example, the German broadcasters were particularly determined to give the campaign in their country a fully European flavour,(6) an emphasis which apparently succeeded in the sense that exceptionally large minorities of German electors did say afterwards that TV programmes: 'showed me where my party stands on European questions'; 'showed me the relationship between Germany's parties and other European parties'; and 'showed me how the European Community is run'. British viewers complained more often than any other national sample about 'feeling rather confused', a natural response of an initially ill-informed public to the much scaled-down campaign that the British broadcasters and politicians organised after having staged a more intensive effort at the earlier general election. Similarly, the numerous complaints of Danish viewers about a 'boring' campaign are conceivably traceable to the night-by-night appearance on that country's sole television channel of a series of 40-minute broadcasts given over in rotation to each of the 12 parties fighting the election (plus the Communists who had put up no candidates of their own).

Viewers were also asked to say whether television had spent 'far too much time' on the European election, 'a bit too much time', 'about the right amount', or 'not enough time'. According to the replies (see Table III.4), campaign 'overkill' was not a major problem, probably reflecting the decisions of many broadcasting organisations to cover the European election less massively than a national one. Only in France, where the last two weeks of the campaign closely resembled a general election pattern, did nearly half the sample complain of 'too much' programming. Those protesting against 'far too much' amounted at most to between a fifth and three-tenths of the electorates - and then only in France, Denmark and Ireland. In general, the countries with more complaints on this score (France, Denmark, Ireland and Germany) were also those where, as reported below, audience members were exposed to a greater volume of election communications. It was also true that in all countries indices of campaign interest were inversely associated with complaints of too much election cover-age: i.e. the latter were voiced chiefly by the less involved respondents. As election argument becomes more obtrusive and difficult to avoid on television, then, it is the less politically minded viewers who complain about having been subjected to 'too much' of it.

A quite different pattern of response to this question was provided by Italian and British viewers, many of whom said that their television networks had paid too little attention to the election. In the former case, this reaction may be explained by the fact that only a week had been allowed for the European campaign after the Italians had voted on the previous Sunday at their national general election. The British response was quite unpre-cedented, for after each of the previous three general elections, approximately two-thirds of the members of national samples complained of 'too much' TV coverage.(7) The viewers' entirely different reaction to the European campaign may have reflected not only their awareness of objectively low levels of party and broadcasting activity, but also some frustration over having been asked to vote in an election with very little information to guide their choice. It is noticeable in this connection that Dutch viewers, who apparently were also exposed to a rather limited campaign but were generally more knowledgeable about European affairs than the British, did not react in the same way.

How did Europeans monitor the campaign?

If an election campaign is to affect the outlook and behaviour of audience members in some way, it must first get through to them. In order economically to collect as much information as possible about the flow of election materials to European voters, respondents were given a card, listing ten different vehicles of campaign communication, with a request to indicate any that they had followed or used 'during the two or three weeks before the European election'. Table III.5, which combines the resulting data into a quantitative index (based on the total number of reported channels of exposure), suggests that the European election campaign reached most voters in the Community through some medium or other - but not often in great quantities. Thus, in five of the eight countries, those claiming not to have been reached by any of the listed means amounted to 13 per cent of the respondents or less - though in Belgium, Britain and the Netherlands about twice that number were 'campaign virgins' in this sense. On the other hand, multi-channel exposure was not very extensive. In six of the eight countries (the exceptions being Germany and Italy), sample majorities recalled receiving campaign material from no more than two media.

The figures in Table III.5 can probably be regarded as an approximate guide to the relative intensity of the communication campaigns that were mounted in the various countries as well. If so, Germany's communication effort was the most vigorous in the Community (except possibly for Italy where technical differences thwart comparison). Electors in Denmark, Ireland and France were exposed to the next most active campaigns. And those put on in Belgium, Britain and the Netherlands were all relatively desultory. It so happens that this rank order tallies quite closely with estimates of their organisations' likely levels of involvement in campaign activity that were independently given to our investigators by party publicity officials interviewed in advance of the election and also with measures, through content analysis, of the overall volume of campaign coverage screened by the various national television services.(8) And (as we shall see in Chapter V), other things being equal, the amount of popular exposure to campaign communications may have impinged on certain election outcomes as well, including voting rates.

Details of exposure to each individual source of election communication are presented in Table III.6. They confirm, for the

40

European election, the significance of television as a political medium of uniquely wide reach, as already established for general elections. In every Community country, more people saw something of the campaign on television than followed it through any other channel. But, in addition, a considerable amount of interpersonal conversation was stimulated by the election. Perhaps its novelty helped to make Europe something of a 'talking point' in many households and work-places. Other media that were mentioned by fairly sizeable minorities included posters, newspaper reports and advertisements. Party literature was read by between a fifth and a third of most sampled electorates. Meetings and rallies played very little part at this election, however, and direct exchanges between electors and party workers were few and far between, except in Ireland and Italy where activists made more effort to contact voters. This may have been due to the proximity of other elections in those countries - held simultaneously for local government councils in Ireland and a week earlier for the national Parliament in Italy. But overall these figures tend to confirm that in many countries party-initiated communication activity was less than full-blooded. Moreover, very few people had tried to persuade others to vote for some particular party at the elections, the numbers involved in such an attempt having ranged from only 4 to 8 per cent of most samples.

Yet another way to gauge how much material about Europe the Community election generated appears in Table III.7. This shows the percentage of each sample who said that they had seen a European news report or programme on televison 'every day', 'nearly every day', 'from time to time' or 'not at all' during 'the two or three weeks before the election'. The figures suggest that, even if most voters were reached by some part of the campaign, their involvement in it was not typically a daily affair. Over television, the most extensively used medium, only minorities ranging from 19 per cent (Belgium) to 36 per cent (Germany) saw European items as often as daily or nearly daily in the last weeks of the campaign.

Table III.8 pursued the distinctive role of television at election time from several other angles. The extreme left-hand column shows the percentages of those voters, who were only a 'little' interested in the campaign, who nevertheless saw something of it on their television screens. This group merits attention, because its members could be presumed to have been in the market for easily available election materials so long as they did not have actively to seek them out - and television is eminently suited to perform the function of supplying material in this way. In fact, in seven of the eight countries, between three-fifths and nine-tenths of this group were exposed to the television campaign. The markedly lower figure for Belgium (44 per cent) probably reflects the ease with which viewers could avoid political programmes in that country, due to the extensive cabling of households and the resulting availability of a wide choice of entertainment programmes from neighbouring nations' networks. The very high exposure rate among the little interested Germans (9 per cent) shows the kind of electoral penetration that may be achieved when a relatively active broadcasting campaign is mounted. The figures are lower, of course, for television exposure by those viewers who were 'not at all interested' in the campaign; but in every country they were still higher for that sub-group than was achieved through any other election vehicle. In Germany, a clear majority of even the 'not at all interested' was reached by the campaign. The right-hand side of the table refers to those individuals who had monitored the campaign through one channel only. It can be seen that in every country television was mentioned most often by the members of this group. But if television did not reach them, then these minimally exposed individuals were most likely to have heard about the campaign in conversations with family members or other acquaintances. And in Ireland political party contacts were also important for a significant minority among them.

Finally, we may ask (as with campaign interest) whether the European election differed greatly from normal general elections in the amount of campaign material that individual voters received through the main media channels. A comparison, based on data taken from the previously mentioned pre-and post-election panel of English electors, is drawn in Table III.9. When consulting these figures, it should be remembered that Britain staged one of the least active campaigns in the entire Community. This need not have affected answers to certain questions, however - about party broadcast viewing, for example, where respondents were asked only about the last programmes of this kind that were transmitted in the week immediately before polling day, or to that about people's levels of attention to election reports whenever they appeared in television news bulletins. The figures show far more audience involvement, via exposure, in the British general election than in the same country's version of the European election. For example, only a third of the sample had read no newspaper story about the general election, compared with three-fifths who recalled no exposure to a press report about the European election. The

42

disparity is even greater for frequency of election conversation in family circles. Most striking, however, are the numbers usually ignoring election reports on television news - two-fifths during the European campaign compared with only a fifth at the time of the general election.

What did voters learn about Europe?

A unique feature of the European election was the necessity it imposed on conscientious and committed communicators patiently to explain to potential voters the workings of certain institutions and processes, with the national equivalents of which most would have been familiar at a general election. This is not the place to describe the resulting efforts in detail, but in broad outline they took four forms. First, to publicists in the employ of the European Commission and Parliament, European consciousness-raising demanded the prior dissemination of Community awareness. So-called 'cognitive mobilisation' (Inglehart, 1977), would be the precursor of transnational identity building and the platform for its development. Consequently, multi-media campaigns designed by advertising agencies were launched in each member country to alert audiences to the impending election, when it was taking place and what it was for; these were timed for cumulative impact throughout the earlier part of 1979 (Lodge and Herman, 1980). Second, to working parties inside the European Broadcasting Union, the election provided an opportunity to plan the screening by all major TV networks of a more or less simultaneously scheduled set of election results programmes on the night of 10 June aiming to underline the European dimension of the voting outcomes as they emerged (Blumler and Petersen, 1981). Third, on to the shoulders of public service broadcasters, the forthcoming election laid a duty to undertake a task of civic education, providing the background information that voters would need so as to follow campaign events and other discussion programmes with at least minimal understanding. The news and current affairs departments of every major television channel accordingly produced a specially prepared series of background programmes and items for the occasion. Varying from network to network in scale and form, this output most often sought to tell audiences about the structure and workings of the European Parliament, to familiarise them with the overall institutional framework of the Common Market, and to show how politicians in the other member countries were fighting the election (Blumler, 1979). Finally, it was assumed that while setting out their wares, the political parties would also be informing voters

43

about some of the issues at the European level that the EEC would have to face in the next five years.

Pursuit of these aims could not be a straightforward matter. The literature of mass communication research includes many examples of informational campaigns that have failed - particularly those dealing with foreign affairs of remote relevance to the daily concerns of audience members (Star and Hughes, 1950; Klapper, 1960; Robinson, 1972). And viewed from the standpoint of many broadcasters, the educative role they were expected to assume was surrounded with pitfalls. For one thing, they had very little to build on in the form of an initial audience grasp of European matters. As a British news editor pointed out when interviewed in early 1979, 'Compared with a general election, we have to start from a much lower level of prior awareness and knowledge in members of the public about European affairs'. For another, audience motivation to attend to informative programming and to learn more about European politics could be weak. As the editor of a BBC-1 current affairs programme put it, 'The European election is important of course, but so far as many members of the public are concerned, they don't really want to know'. To some broadcasters low levels of audience interest also implied that European programming should not be overdone. An all-out effort would be disproportionate: 'The audience would not thank us if we tried to ply them with a lot of material on Europe or tried to get them to concentrate their minds on European issues at the forthcoming election'. Moreover, since broadcasters lacked guidelines on how best to discharge their informational functions for Europe, they tended to fall back on already familiar production styles. For example, asked what explanatory items his bulletin might present during the campaign, a British television news editor mentioned three possible topics:

i) How the other European countries are treating the European election and conducting their campaigns.
ii) Features on interesting personalities involved in those campaigns.
iii) How European Community policies that affect people in this country are perceived in the other countries.

This reply illustrates the tendency of a journalist to make a novel task manageable by assimilating it to customary professional routines - in this case to the familiar news-value criteria of curiosity, personalisation and relevance. Whether such an approach would advance audience awareness of European affairs, however, he had no means of knowing.(9)

And what exactly was accomplished as a result of those several efforts? Some impressions can be formed by drawing on three sources of evidence: responses before and after the campaign to a few knowledge questions put to panels of voters in Britain, Germany and the Netherlands; answers to a question about the voting results put to respondents in the eight-nation post-election survey; and answers from the same individuals to a question about the issues of the election.

Changes of knowledge level

The measurement of political knowledge in opinion polling is hazardous. There is no agreement over what a well-informed citizen should know about any level of government, and investigators are naturally anxious not to make respondents feel like students undergoing an examination. In each of the panel studies that were fielded in Britain, Germany and the Netherlands, only a limited attempt was made to survey voter's grasp of Community questions, and Table III.10 summarises the scatter of findings that was obtained.(10)

The results convey an impression of large boulders having been painfully pushed up a steep incline, so that at the end of the day some were perched marginally higher up the slope than before the campaign opened. In fact, on every point of information about which the panel members were questioned knowledge levels did rise somewhat over the campaign period, and certain measured gains were associated to a statistically significant extent with some form of exposure to the campaign. But people more readily absorbed information if it had domestic relevance (the names of party list leaders in the Netherlands and of constituency candidates in Britain) than if it concerned the Community as such (e.g. questions about EEC member states, the Parliament's powers, the Community budget, etc.) or the campaign that was waged in other countries. The evidence also underlines the unrealism of expecting a campaign of short duration to transform an already quite uninformed populace into a highly knowledgeable one. The table not only discloses a big contrast between the prior awareness of Dutchmen and Englishmen, but also shows that, even after the campaign was over, only a minority of Britons (not exceeding 38 per cent on any point) knew the correct answers to the questions put in the interviews. Indeed, some of the British results stand out as a spectacular tribute to the country's impervious insularity.

Awareness of the election results

In the eight-nation survey an attempt was made to measure the acquisition of knowledge about the election results. This, it was felt, was a form of information which would emerge directly from media coverage of the election and be common in all the member countries. In domestic elections such a question would be unlikely to pose any problems for voters. The election result, measured by the relative success of the contending parties and the fate of governments, is a prime focus of media attention and the culmination of their coverage of the campaign. In all Community countries substantial resources and professional effort are invested in first predicting, and then monitoring in detail, the election outcome. In the first European election the television programmes on the results were similarly to be the climax of campaign coverage, albeit at lower levels. But our question on the election outcome revealed a dramatic picture of widespread ignorance and confusion. The question focused on the result at the European level and asked:

> Leaving aside which party did best here in (country name), do you know which group of parties won the largest number of seats in the European Parliament as a whole?

Respondent's replies to this question are shown in Table III.11. Two impressions emerge forcefully from this evidence. First, large numbers of respondents were unable to provide any answer to the question. In two Community countries, one in three declared themselves unable to answer; in four others, the figure was one in two, and in Ireland, it exceeded two in three. Second, among those offering replies, the patterns of response diverged markedly from country to country. In only two countries - Italy and Denmark - did a majority of those giving answers correctly name the Socialists as the party with the largest number of seats (and in the Danish case this majority was quite marginal). German electors were the most confident that they knew the result of the election but split their replies, in the main, between the Socialist Group and the Christian Democrats. French electors who offered an answer were similarly divided; and in other cases the patterns of response suggested a confusion of the European result with the one at home. In Britain, for example, the largest single category of response declared that the European Conservatives(11) had won the largest number of seats, and in Belgium and the Netherlands respondents tended to choose the Christian Democratic Group.

What significance should be attached to these findings and the evident confusion they reveal? With hindsight we are reluctant to see them as an entirely satisfactory test of electors' knowledge of the election result; there were other outcomes to the election which could have been clearer to respondents than the specific focus of our question. There are at least two reasons for this. First, the outcome of the election, so far as the leading contenders were concerned, was closer at the European level than had been generally predicted and allowed for differing interpretations of success and failure. For example, though the Socialist Group won the most seats, the Christian Democrats attracted more popular votes; while, compared to their strengths in the old Parliament, the former had lost seats and the latter had gained. There was, then, a sense of ambiguity about the election outcome. This is not to argue that the details of this ambiguity were understood by respondents but merely to suggest that there was in the reported election results room for alternative understandings of success and failure. Second, in the European context, the focus of our question is much less significant politically than it would be in an election for a national Parliament. Though the Socialists comprised the largest group in the new Parliament, they won only 27 per cent of the total number of seats. Moreover, no executive depended on their votes and no change of course emanated from it. There was political significance in the overall prominence in the Parliament of Centre-Right members but little or none in the fortunes of particular groups.

Nevertheless, the distribution of seats among party groups was an outcome of the election, and our question was specific. The fact that few Europeans were able to answer it correctly indicates widespread ignorance and confusion at the European level.(12) To a large extent this must reflect the sparse attention paid to the results at the European level by broadcasting and other media services and their focus on voting at the national level. This is perhaps clearest in the Irish case, where the lengthy requirements of vote-counting led to a prolongation of suspense over the national result and its declaration long after the result at the European level was 'known'. As a consequence less than 10 per cent of the Irish electors were aware of the outcome sought in our question and less than one-third even attempted a reply to it.

Awareness of election issues
    Low levels of awareness and divergent patterns of response are also key features of our data on respondents' recognition of

47

election issues. We tend to take it for granted that national elections will pivot on certain widely diffused and commonly recognised focal points of choice, and that these include a set of policy issues regarded as urgent for incoming governments to tackle. Campaign communications from politicians and journalists repeatedly play on and highlight a defined (if somewhat emergent) agenda of public issues, together with party images, records of achievement and the leadership qualities regarded as necessary to cope with the issues. In part, this agenda is established in advance of the election; in part, journalists and politicians struggle to shape it during the campaign. However it comes about - a topic to which much attention is currently being paid by students of the so-called agenda-setting process (Shaw and McCombs, 1977; Weaver, et al., 1981) - the product provides a common framework to guide publicists' efforts and to focus voters' perceptions of the choices before them. In the European Community, however, such a framework was, at best, fragmented in 1979.

Our evidence on perceptions of issues during the European campaign is presented in Table III.12. We asked respondents:

What do you think were the most important issues that emerged during the European elections?

Spontaneous replies were coded by interviewers according to the categories listed in the table, and anyone able to mention an issue was further asked, 'Anything else?', until he or she could think of no more.

The inability of a large number of Europeans to associate even a single issue with the electoral choice before them is clearly apparent in the penultimate line of the table. Those totally unaware of any specific issue ranged from 22 per cent in Germany and Ireland, through a little under 30 per cent in France and the Netherlands, to 42 per cent in Italy, 51 per cent in Britain, and around 60 per cent in Belgium and Denmark; and in the last four countries 'don't know' constituted the largest category of response. Lack of issue awareness and voting abstention also appear to be linked, for among non-voters the proportions unable to nominate an issue rose to between 41 per cent and 73 per cent. For many electors, then, the agenda-setting process never even got started in the first Community election. Many voters emerged from the experience with a blank agenda paper.

The second feature of this evidence is the cross-national variety of response among those able to identify an issue emerging in the campaign. That is, no common election agenda prevailed among the issue-conscious sectors of the European electorate. Thus in Belgium and France, unemployment was most frequently nominated as an election issue, while in Italy pecedence was given to inflation and rising prices. The Irish showed approximately equal levels of concern with inflation, unemployment and agri-culture, while the Danes focused on their country's membership of the Community and the case for staying in or leaving. In Britain the key issue was the Community's agricultural policies, while the Dutch opted for unemployment, energy policies and the need to promote more European co-operation. German electors were unique in mentioning the need for further co-operation more often than any other issue and also, to a lesser extent, for seeing the election in terms of rival ideological visions of the future of Europe - i.e. whether it should be a Socialist Europe or a Christian Democratic one.

In presenting this evidence on issue awareness we have drawn attention to its similarities with knowledge of the election result. In both cases the findings indicate patterns of widespread ignor-ance and cross-national divergence. But whereas the result of the election was a potentially common item of knowledge across the Community, knowledge of issues was not. The national campaigns gave rise to different issues and it is the recognition of these differences that is reflected in the second part of these findings. In a sense, despite the high proportions of blank agenda papers, the figures do suggest the presence of recognisable, if somewhat sparse, national agendas. Thus, in Belgium and France, among those identifying an issue, unemployment was mentioned by 50 and 56 per cent of the respondents, respectively. In Germany, 40 per cent of those identifying issues nominated co-operation and in Britain 45 per cent opted for agricultural policies. Similar national preoccupations emerged in other countries, which implied that among the aware there was a convergence toward national consen-sus on the key issue(s) of the campaign. National campaigns, therefore, not surprisingly tended to produce national issue agendas.

But whatever is said about the organisation of the first European election campaigns, this was more than a national election. It was international and was designed to select an international Parliament, and in that context the absence of a

European issue-agenda is significant. As we have previously noted, part of the role of the election, as seen by its originators, was to stimulate European consciousness and co-operation. Added to this, commentators saw in the election a potential for legitimising the government structures of the European Community. A democratically elected Parliament could claim popular support for its actions and decisions. And yet, it is difficult to see in our findings on the issues of the election much support for these ideas. With the exceptions of Germany and the Netherlands, there appears to be little recognition that the election was about greater European co-operation - nor, for that matter, that it was concerned with defending national independence and culture against supranationalism. Neither is there much recognition that the election was about democratising the institutions of the Community. In all countries fewer than five per cent saw democratic control of Europe and its bureaucracy or the powers of the Parliament as election issues. For the most part the issues that emerged in the first campaigns for the Parliament tended to be more concrete - even of a 'bread-and-butter' character. This is not to say that they were non-European (though in a number of cases they probably reflected reactions to domestic politics and domestic government performances), but they were in a sense 'national' concerns. British electors, for example, showed a decided preoccupation with agricultural issues, which was clearly a concern about European agricultural policies. It represented, that is, an 'ethnocentric' relationship to European politics, not a merely domestic perspective.

We opened this section with a comment on the role of issue agendas in national elections. We there implied that, in identifying the problems which governments are expected to face with urgency, such core campaign issues do set the agenda, initially at least, for subsequent government and parliamentary activity. Clearly, parallels between national Parliaments and the European Parliament should not be over-emphasised, but the fragmented character of the Community issue agenda in 1979 implies that at that time there was very little consensus over what the European Parliament should concern itself with, let alone how it should tackle the problems of Europe. For the Parliament to acquire authority as a democratic institution, deriving its legitimacy from the Community's electorate, high turn-out figures would not be enough. It requires also a more or less common public expectation that it will fulfil tasks appropriate to it which are seen as important by those who elected it. The absence of a Community-wide issue agenda in 1979 is therefore significant in that there was no agreement on the priorities by which the parliamentarians should be guided following their election.

At later elections (1984 and beyond) comparisons of voters' impressions of European issues with the 1979 reactions reported above should be sought. They could provide a revealing measure of any progress made at the public opinion level towards further European Community integration.

A summary cross-national comparison of electoral involvement

In many respects the European election campaigns of 1979 seemed quite similar everywhere. Typically, they agitated few voters' pulses, exciting little interest; they were fairly easily avoided by those not wanting to become involved; their presentation on television elicited a mixed and lukewarm reaction at best; and out of the mix of party statements and mass media reports that comprised each national campaign, it was difficult to form a clear impression of the issues facing the Common Market. Nevertheless, the various campaigns were also distinctive in certain ways that were not always predictable from particular countries' past relationships to the European Community.

Table III.13 shows how seven of the countries (omitting Italy due to measurement incompatibility) can be ranked according to each of five indicators of European election involvement plus one for level of public approval of Common Market membership. When they are listed in this way, some countries manifest a rather consistent pattern of response to the first Community election, while others show a less even reaction. Germany stands out in the former camp as having experienced the most invigorating election in almost all respects measured; that is, the German electors were highest in campaign interest, exposure and evaluation, and in voting turn-out, and they performed creditably as regards issue awareness as well. The Irish campaign (possibly propped by the simultaneous local government election) was also rather consistently involving. Although few Irishmen claimed to have been keenly interested in the campaign, they followed it quite extensively, rated its TV coverage fairly positively, had quite a lot to offer on the election issues, and went to the polls in reasonable numbers. At the other extreme, the Belgian and British efforts elicited consistently low-key responses from many electors, who tended to lack interest in the campaign, followed it only cursorily,

51

gave low marks to its TV coverage and had little to say when asked about the issues. More mixed patterns marked people's responses in the other countries. Although the French were moderately high in campaign interest, exposure, issue awareness and turn-out, they were not at all impressed with the television version of their election, which they criticised more severely on a number of counts than did viewers elsewhere. For their part, the Dutch recorded low rates of exposure to a campaign to which they otherwise responded with moderate interest, few evaluations of any kind and a high level of abstentions; yet they scored well above the European average as regards issue awareness. A unique dynamic also shaped the campaign in Denmark. Comparatively high in initial interest and follow-up exposure, many Danes reacted to the election with disappointment in the end - as if it had finally proved stultifyingly narrow in issue focus and far less worthy of voting participation than any general election would have been.

It is also intriguing to see how the various countries are positioned when the batting orders for electoral involvement are compared with the national rankings for EEC membership approval. Particularly striking is the lack of any sign that campaign interest, exposure or evaluation were functions of high electoral regard for the European Community. Whereas the sceptical Danes fought a fairly spirited contest, the more supportive Belgians and Dutch undertook a less committed effort. Where these indices happened to coincide, however, the main election outcomes (such as voting rates and levels of issue awareness) tended to follow suit. For example, the pro-European Germans, who staged a relatively active campaign, also managed to name election issues and turned out at the polls in above-average numbers. Britain offers an example of such a consistent pattern in reverse. With few enthusiasts for Community membership, and having undergone a lack-lustre campaign, her electors could think of few issues that had emerged from the exercise and very often declined the opportunity to vote. The deviant cases (in this sense) of the Netherlands and Belgium clearly highlight the risks involved in not taking the campaign seriously. For, despite high levels of public acceptance of the Community, turn-out in the former country, and issue awareness in the latter, were low. Moreover, as we saw in Chapter II, the desultory campaigns in both these countries appeared to reduce the number of committed supporters of Common Market membership. However, more vigorous campaigning did not always compensate for an electorate's indifference or antagonism to the EEC. In doubtful Denmark, for example, many electors abstained from voting and could think of no issue which had emerged from the campaign, despite the relatively energetic party and broadcasting efforts that were mounted there.

NOTES

1. Some of the material presented in this chapter and Chapter IV first appeared in Blumler and Fox (1980).

2. The results of empirical tests of these suggestions about the possibly pivotal role of campaign interest may be found in Chapter V.

3. The British panel survey was conducted in the European parliamentary constituencies of Bristol and Manchester North West. 444 respondents were interviewed after the general election on 3 May, and 372 of them were re-interviewed after the European election. The survey was jointly funded by the BBC and the Independent Broadcasting Authority, and the interviews were carried out on the authors' behalf by the BBC Audience Research Department.

4. That filter excluded between a fifth and a third of the sample members in seven countries - though not in Germany where only 7 per cent had failed to follow the campaign on television at all.

5. Even in Italy, where each item was presented to sample members for separate consideration, only 13 per cent claimed to have derived voting guidance from the campaign.

6. Of a sample of German TV journalists 63 per cent expected to put on a predominantly 'European' (as opposed to a more 'domestic') campaign. In no other national sample of broadcasters interviewed on identical lines before the campaign opened did the equivalent expectation exceed 33 per cent.

7. The evidence may be found in The Coverage of the 1979 General Election Campaign on Television and Radio, British Broadcasting Corporation, London, 1981, Part 2, and The Coverage of the 1974 General Election Campaign on Television and Radio, British Broadcasting Corporation, London, 1974.

8. The national ranks referred to in the text were as follows:

Samples' overall campaign exposure	Index of political party motivation to fight a keen campaign	Volume of campaign coverage on TV (No. of programme minutes
1 Germany	1 Ireland	1 Netherlands
2 Ireland	2 France	2 Germany
3 Denmark	3 Germany	3 France
4 France	4 Denmark	4 Denmark
5 Belgium	5 Belgium	5 Belgium
6 Britain	6 Britain	6 Britain
7 Netherlands	7 Netherlands	7 Ireland

The association between the party motivation index and the samples' reported campaign exposure levels is exceptionally strong. National differences in volume of TV programming were less clearly related to electors' exposure rates, due chiefly to 'misplacements' of the Netherlands and Ireland. But the Dutch position was artifically boosted by the number of long documentary programmes scheduled in off-peak hours, while in Ireland the relative intensity of party commitments to a predominantly domestic campaign apparently overrode to some extent the decision of RTE to organise a low-key programming effort (Feeney, 1979).

9. This material is drawn from Blumler, 1979.

10. The German results appeared in Schonbach and Schulz, 1980. The Dutch results are analysed in an unpublished report by McQuail and Davis, 1980.

11. The European Conservative group changed its name between the period of the election and the first sitting of the new Parliament to the European Democratic group.

12. There may be an additional source of confusion in the term 'group', which may account for some of the 'European Conservative' replies to this question. Britain and Denmark - the two countries contributing MEPs to the group - clearly have the largest proportions of electors offering this reply. But the equivalent numbers in France, Germany and Ireland are not entirely negligible for a group ranked third in the Parliament with 64 seats to the Socialists' 112 and the

Christian Democrats' 108. But of those 64 seats, 61 derive from the British Conservative Party and these make up the largest single national party contingent in the Parliament. In the absence of knowledge of EP groupings, the (British) Conservatives could well have appeared to some respondents as the largest group in the Parliament.

Table III.1   Interest in the European election campaign

Percentages

	B	Dk	F	G	GB	Irl	I	NI
Very interested	7	14	9	6	9	15	6	7
Quite interested	19	25	30	40	21	18	23	29
Only a little interested	26	36	33	38	28	30	43	33
Not at all interested	43	23	27	15	41	33	28	27
Don't know/ No reply	5	2	1	1	1	4	0	4
Total N	(965)	(1,018)	(1,002)	(807)	(914)	(1,276)	(985)	(1,159)

Table III.2   Comparisons of interest in British general and European election campaigns

How interesting did you find the recent general election campaign?		How interesting did you find the campaign leading up to the European election?
%		%
20	Very interesting	3
32	Fairly interesting	13
22	Slightly interesting	32
24	Not at all interesting	47
2	Don't know	5
100		100

N = 372

Table III.3   Evaluation of television coverage of the European election campaign[a]

Percentages

	B	Dk	F	G	GB	Irl	Nl
			Overall ratings				
Per cent endorsing one or more negative statements	61	63	67	64	62	55	54
Per cent endorsing one or more positive statements	46	54	47	66	43	57	46
			Endorsement of individual statements				
Negative statements Television coverage:							
all seemed rather boring	21	32	23	29	19	18	14
did not show the advantages and disadvantages of Community membership	30	21	31	30	20	18	22
left me feeling rather confused	19	29	30	11	34	28	10
did not show why I should care about European Parliament	13	18	13	30	15	16	16
Positive statements Television coverage:							
helped me think more about the future of Europe	18	20	13	21	17	21	15
showed me where my party stands on European questions	13	27	17	34	15	19	9
showed the main differences between the parties	15	19	23	22	12	14	7
showed me the relationship between (country's) parties and other European parties	16	10	12	24	9	16	12
showed me how the EC is run	11	11	8	25	13	15	11
helped me decide how to vote	10	10	9	13	10	17	5
Total (N)	(520)	(811)	(724)	(755)	(630)	(876)	(820)

a   The administration of similar statements to Italian sample members was too different to allow comparison with responses from the other countries.

Table III.4   Evaluations of the total amount of campaign coverage on television[a]

Percentages

	B	Dk	F	G	GB	Irl	I	Nl
Time devoted to European election campaign was:								
Far too much	14	21	29	12	9	19	13	13
A bit too much	18	10	20	24	9	22	10	16
About the right amount	46	45	38	54	30	45	34	47
Not enough	11	9	5	8	43	13	42	18
Don't know/No reply	11	15	8	2	9	1	1	6
Total N	(5200	(811)	(723)	(755)	(630)	(876)	(735)	(820)

a   The question was put to those seeing European programmes or news reports on TV at least 'from time to time' during the campaign.

59

Table III.5   Exposure to the European election campaign: number of channels through which communication received

Percentages

	B	Dk	F	G	GB	Irl	I[a]	Nl
Number of channels:								
0	22	10	13	3	23	11	6	23
1	30	25	24	15	25	25	10	29
2	13	18	21	20	18	21	11	16
3	13	14	16	16	12	15	13	12
4	8	12	10	15	7	8	14	9
5	5	7	7	10	6	8	14	4
6	4	6	4	10	4	5	12	3
7	3	5	2	6	3	4	8	2
8	1	2	1	3	2	1	6	1
9	0	1	1	1	0	2	3	1
10	1	0	1	1	0	-	3	0
Total N	(965)	(1,018)	(1,002)	(795)	(914)	(1,276)	(985)	(1,159)

a.   More numerous Italian responses are probably due to two factors: the recency of the country's general election (one week before European polling) and its communication campaign; administration of each item individually to the respondents.

60

Table III.6   Exposure to individual channels of European election communication

Percentages

	B	Dk	F	G	GB	Irl	I	NI
Talked to friends, family or workmates	29	48	46	54	33	39	59	35
Spoke to a political party worker	4	4	8	8	5	30	24	4
Attended a public meeting or rally	2	2	4	9	2	9	17	2
Read election materials sent to my house	22	19	28	33	25	33	46	18
Read a poster about the European election	34	29	24	45	17	36	65	14
Read an advertisement in a newspaper about the election	28	40	21	49	19	35	53	24
Read a newspaper report about the election	24	44	28	48	36	(a)	44	39
Watched a programme about the election on TV	46	71	65	77	54	54	73	44
Heard a programme about the election on radio	18	21	30	33	19	30	30	17
Tried to persuade somebody to vote for a party in the election	5	8	5	8	7	4	22	5
Total N	965	1,018	1,002	795	914	1,276	985	1,159

a   Omitted from the Irish survey.

Table III.7   Exposure to the European election campaign: Frequency of watching television programmes and news reports about the election

Percentages

	B	Dk	F	G	GB	Irl	I	NI
Watched television programmes and news reports:								
Every day	8	14	16	4	12	11	8	9
Nearly every day	11	21	13	32	13	14	16	18
From time to time	35	45	43	57	44	44	13a 38a	44
Not at all	41	19	26	6	31	28	25	28
Don't know/ No reply	5	1	2	1	0	3	-	1
Total N =	(965)	(1,018)	(1,002)	(795)	(914)	(1,276)	(985)	(1,159)

a Italian response alternatives: Every day, nearly every day, two or three times a week, less than that, not at all?

Table III.8   Importance of television among less interested and little exposed voters

	Per cent seeing some TV among: 'little interested'	'not interested'	Per cent exposed to TV among singlechannel users	2nd most important channel among single-channel users (Per cent)	
Belgium	44	33	41	Conversations	(18)
Denmark	72	41	55	Conversations	(26)
France	61	45	51	Conversations	(28)
Germany	91	58	38	Conversations	(22)
Great Britain	67	38	48	Conversations	(20)
Ireland	62	37	26	Conversations	(23)[a]
Italy	62	45	43	Read a poster	(21)
Netherlands	63	24	30	Conversations	(24)

a   Also mentioned: 12 per cent talked to party workers; 12 per cent read election literature.

Table III.9   Comparison of British exposure to election communications

Percentages

	General election	European election
Read newspaper election reports:		
Most days	34	8
2-3 days	22	15
Less	10	19
None	33	59
Talked about election in family:		
Most days	38	9
2-3 days	23	13
Less	14	20
None	25	58
Election reports on TV news:		
Usually ignored	19	40
Followed fairly closely	65	54
Followed very closely	16	4
Don't know	1	3
Final Party broadcasts:		
Saw Conservative broadcast	46	30
Saw Labour broadcast	55	26
Saw Liberal broadcast	43	25

Table III.10   Campaign-period knowledge gains recorded by before-and-after panels in three countries

Percentages

	Before	After
NETHERLANDS		
Knew the election was for a <u>Community</u> Parliament	60	73
Ability to designate EEC countries (average across countries)	60	76
Ability to identify leaders of five party lists (average)	32	64
Knew number of Dutch seats in European Parliament (approx)	6	62
BRITAIN (Bristol and Manchester)		
Heard something about Parliament's powers	22	27
Knew agriculture was the largest item in the EEC budget	27	36
Knew name of their constituency	4	27
Knew name of at least one constituency candidate	2	38
Could name a European Party allied to the Conservative Party	1	5
Could name a European Party allied to the Labour Party	4	17
Could name a European Party allied to the Liberal Party	1	5
Could name a politician fighting the campaign in another Community country	2	12
GERMANY		
Knew number of German seats in European Parliament (approx)	5	18

65

Table III.11   Perceptions of party victors of the European election overall

Percentages

	B	Dk	F	G	GB	Irl	I	NI
Communists and Allies	-	-	1	1	0	1	1	0
Socialists	14	26	19	41	12	9	44	22
Liberal & Democratic Group	3	6	2	3	1	3	1	3
Christian Democrats	32	6	16	38	7	15	19	32
European Con- servatives	1	10	4	6	29	4	2	2
European Progressive Democrats	1	0	5	a	0	2	a	2
Others	1	3	3	1	2	1	a	1
Don't know	48	50	50	11	48	67	33	38
Total N =	(1,007)	(1,035)	(1,002)	(807)	(925)	(1,280)	(985)	(1,159)

a   Response categories not included in German and Italian questionnaires.

66

Table III.12   Perception of European election issues

Percentages

	B	Dk	F	G	GB	Irl	I	NI
Unemployment, jobs, work opportunities	20	2	40	2	3	31	11	36
Prices, inflation, cost of living	6	-	12	-	12	32	19	13
Agricultural policy, fishing, food mountains	2	3	8	0	22	27	9	13
Energy, nuclear power, conservation	12	3	9	4	2	15	16	33
Greater European co-operation, unity, avoidance of war	8	5	6	31	6	5	12	23
Protection of national sovereignty, independence, culture	-	4	8	-	1	2	1	4
Stronger democratic control over EC, powers of EP, control of bureaucracy	1	1	2	4	3	3	1	5
Regional and urban development, regional fund, regional needs	2	-	2	-	1	7	4	2
Social policies, human rights, status of women and minorities	1	-	4	2	-	7	1	9
International relations, Europe's relations with other powers and Third World	1	-	5	3	2	4	1	9
Political preferences for Europe, the ideological future of Europe	1	2	2	16	2	2	3	6
Other issues	7	26a	24	24	8	5	8	-
Don't know/No reply	59	62	29	22	51	22	42	27
Don't know/No reply among non-voters	72	73	41	45	66	41	59	41

a   Chiefly responses about the pros and cons of Community membership per se.

Table III.13   Rankings of seven Community countries on selected indicators of campaign involvement and Community opinion

Interest	Communic-ation exposure	TV campaign evaluation	Issue awareness	Turn-out as per cent of GE rate	EEC Membership 'good thing' (June 1979)
Germany	Germany	Germany	Netherlands	Germany	Netherlands
Denmark	Denmark	Ireland	Ireland	Ireland	Germany
France	Ireland	Denmark	Germany	France	Belgium
Netherlands	France	Netherlands	France	Netherlands	France
Ireland	Britain	Belgium	britain	Denmark	Ireland
Britain	Belgium	Britain	Belgium	Britain	Denmark
Belgium	Netherlands	France	Denmark		Britain

IV THE UNEVEN REACH OF THE CAMPAIGN

In the previous chapter we discussed the responses of national electorates to a predominantly low-key set of elections. Now we turn to lines of cleavage within mass publics, tracing the differential reception of the campaign by various electoral sub-groups. For this purpose, we focus on two expressions of involvement featured in Chapter III - interest in the campaign and exposure to it - and add to them a third measure, turn-out on polling day.(1) In short, we ask: Who was involved? Who voted? Which groups reacted most enthusiastically to the campaign? Whom did it leave untouched? At issue in this analysis is the potential of a Community election to disseminate the European message more widely into the ranks of formerly less perceptive citizens. Three types of categories are examined in pursuit of these questions: attitudinal groups, identified by people's opinions on Community membership and the prospective impact of the Parliament; demographic groups, defined by respondents' sex, age or education; and political groups, based on electors' party preferences.

There were good reasons to expect such groups to be unevenly reached by the campaign. We have already mentioned the possibility that supporters of the Community would participate more actively than its opponents and sceptics - though reactions might also depend on the kind of lead given by politicians to holders of such opinions during the campaign. Levels of involvement might also turn on people's demographic traits. Past studies of political behaviour have often documented variations in the participation rates of men and women, younger and older electors, and individuals from different educational backgrounds - especially in 'weak-stimulus elections' (Crewe, 1981). Yet the novelty of the European campaign might have awakened fresh responses in some of these categories.   Finally, if the incentives for the parties to throw themselves fully into the European fray were less clear-cut than usual, a differential mobilisation of their supporters was a likely consequence.

Although we have referred to these categories as 'groups', they do not, of course, form discretely bounded social entities. Individuals combine within themselves the characteristics, roles and viewpoints which we treat here in some isolation from each other. In the next chapter we shall try to assess the relative weight of these factors (in conjunction with others) in stimulating involvement in the 1979 election.   Here our aim is to provide a broad sketch of the campaign's penetration into several major social and political sectors of the population.

Attitudes to Europe

On the whole those voters who were favourably disposed to the European Community were more actively involved in the 1979 campaign than those who were sceptical, indifferent or opposed to their country's membership. The evidence of the post-election surveys confirms that Community supporters were more likely to have been interested in following the campaign and to have monitored it more extensively, and were more likely to have voted than those taking other views.   Yet the relationship between 'Europeanism' in this sense and electoral participation was also more complex than these preliminary generalisations imply.

Table IV.1 shows how those adopting different attitudes to Common Market membership responded to the European election. In every country, those believing membership to be a 'good thing' displayed the highest level of interest in the campaign. But in three countries, opponents were almost as interested as the Community's supporters in Belgium and Italy, where admittedly they were numerically insignificant, and in Denmark where they formed a more sizeable block. And in all countries except Britain, opponents showed a keener interest than those occupying what we have previously termed the 'middle ground'. When involvement was measured by exposure to the campaign (the average number of channels through which individuals received election information), supporters and opponents often appeared more alike. It is true that in Germany, Ireland and Britain, pro-Europeans were clearly reached by more channels of communication than were the anti-

Marketeers. But in Denmark that pattern was actually reversed, and in France, Italy and the Netherlands, opponents were at least as involved as supporters in this respect. Britain again stands out as the only country where opponents were less likely to have participated than even those who considered the Community 'neither good nor bad'. On turn-out, however, the tendency for pro-Europeans to become more involved emerged more strongly. With the exception of Denmark, the gap between Community supporters and opponents widened considerably, and the voting participation of those regarding membership as a 'bad thing' often fell below that of electors who felt undecided about the Community's worth. In France, Germany and Ireland, turn-out among opponents was nearly 20 per cent lower than among supporters, and in the Netherlands and Britain the differences increased to 27 per cent and 37 per cent, respectively. Indeed, in Britain those who were clear in their minds that Market membership was a 'bad thing' abstained even more frequently than did the 'don't knows' (who elsewhere were usually less inclined to vote than were respondents in any other opinion category).

The lower turn-out rates for opponents of Community member-ship are not surprising. A variety of explanations could apply, ranging from objections in principle to voting for a European Parliament, through difficulties in accommodating personal positions on Europe to the pro-market stance of parties normally supported, to a sense of futility in voting for minority anti-European parties or candidates where such opportunities were presented.(2) In any case, this shortfall usually lacked electoral significance, given the limited strength of opponents in the older Community states. But in two countries - Britain and Denmark - they constituted major electoral fractions which, as we have seen, responded very differently to the European campaign. In Denmark, the anti-Marketeers were relatively well mobilised. They were more often reached by the campaign than any other Danish group, as likely to have been interested in it, and as likely to have voted. In Britain, the reverse was true. Most opponents were campaign 'drop-outs' - least interested in the campaign, least attentive to it, and least likely to have voted. These differences are largely traceable to the political organisation of the two campaigns. In Denmark the 1979 election threw up an inter-party (though Left-dominated) protest movement against Danish membership of the Community, which revived the whole issue of the country's place in Europe. This 'People's Movement' provided political leadership for opposition sentiments and captured the second largest share of the

Danish vote. Moreover, its 'cross-party' character allowed opponents of the Community to vote according to their European opinions without incurring guilt over betraying loyalties that might have been aroused by other forms of vote-switching. Thus, one in five of those Social Democratic respondents who cast ballots voted for the People's Movement rather than for their own party, and though the greater part of its support stemmed from left-of-centre parties, our evidence shows that some voters were drawn to this coalition from all quarters of the Danish party spectrum. Nothing comparable happened in Britain. Labour, the party which was most critical of Europe and was traditionally supported by the more convinced anti-Marketeers, was internally divided over its European policy line and had long been plagued by uncertainty over whether, and how, to fight the election (Butler and Marquand, 1981). Moreover, had it tried to mount a vigorous anti-Community campaign, it is unlikely that it could have attracted many supporters of other parties (though it might have galvanised more of its own partisans) so soon after a domestic general election in which it had lost power.

Thus, the impact of attitudes to the Community on levels of campaign involvement varied markedly from country to country. As we have seen, the Danish campaign produced a polarised pattern, which encouraged an even mobilisation of supporters and opponents alike, while leaving many holders of 'middle-ground' opinions on the sidelines. In Britain, there was a highly skewed pattern: the pro-Marketeers were quite actively involved in the campaign (reacting more like their counterparts in the other countries than like most of their fellow nationals), but participation rates fell away sharply in the rest of the population as opinions became less positive. In the remaining countries, the patterns varied according to the measure of involvement examined. On turn-out there was generally a skewed distribution in favour of the Community's supporters and against its opponents; but though there were similar skews in Germany, Ireland and the Netherlands on interest, and in Germany and Ireland on exposure, there was much less differentiation between supporters and opponents in the other Community states. In France, the rather shallow involvement gradients across opinion groups may have reflected the political content of a campaign which, though largely conducted by parties that supported membership of the Community, was nevertheless critical of its development, defensive of French interests, and widely regarded as a test of the contenders' domestic popularity (Hollick, 1979).(3) In Belgium and Italy, however, overall levels

72

of interest in the 1979 campaign were low in comparison with the rest of the Community, and an explanation of the relative lack of differentiation by opinion there may reside in the fact that the campaign made little impact on anyone.

It should not be assumed, however, that, so far as attitudinal influences on involvement are concerned, only people's views on the benefits of EEC membership mattered. Since the election focused much attention on the European Parliament as an institution, those who felt that it was, or could become, a significant political force could have been prepared to take the campaign more seriously - regardless of their opinions about Community membership.

To tap such perceptions, it will be recalled that we asked our sample members the following question:

Thinking about the future, how much effect do you think what the European Parliament does will have on people like yourself - a great effect, some effect, not much effect, or no effect at all?

Table IV.2 shows how these different estimates of the likely impact of the Parliament's activities in the future were associated with people's responses to the European campaign. In fact the involvement differences between those expecting the Parliament to have a 'great' effect on the lives of Europeans and those expecting to have 'no' effect are dramatically large. With only minor qualifications in the Dutch results, the association is clear, strong and consistent: the more individuals believed that the new Parliament would affect people like themselves, the more interested they were in the campaign, the more closely they followed it through all available communication channels, and the more likely they were to have voted. Replies to this question actually differentiated the involved from the indifferent voters more successfully than did opinions on the benefits of Community membership in all countries except Britain.

The importance of these perceptions can be demonstrated by examining their role in those countries where the other opinion question was not all that successful in discriminating between the more and less involved electors - namely, in Belgium, Denmark, France and Italy. Figures for these countries, showing the association with campaign interest and exposure of both opinion about

73

Community membership and impressions of the Parliament's relevance, when each is held constant against the other, are presented in Table IV.3. It can be seen that in all four countries, for each statement of opinion about the value of community membership, those who rated the Parliament's future impact more highly were consistently, and often by wide margins more actively involved in the election than were those who expected its influence to be insignificant.

In sum, the first direct election to the European Parliament was more than a mere celebration of Europe by the faithful. In certain circumstances opponents of the Community were also engaged participants (though voting came less easily to some of them). And in even greater measure the 1979 campaign had a special hold on those who saw the election as a meaningful political act, in the sense that the Parliament's decisions could be relevant to their lives in the future.

Demographic influences on involvement
Sex

A poster prepared for the Community's pre-election information campaign showed nine cartoon figures of women, each carrying her national flag, and bore the caption, 'Women of Europe Have Your Say'. This exhortation to a specific category of Europeans expected a lower level of participation among women - as had been predicted in pre-election reports (Eurobarometre, No.11, May 1979). And yet women were far from absent from the 1979 campaigns. A number figured predominantly in their parties' lists of candidates and in national and international media coverage. In addition, the proportion of women elected was higher than in corresponding national Parliaments in all countries except Belgium where they remained the same (Kohn, 1981). And Mme Simone Veil emerged from the first session of the new Parliament as its elected president. These were not dramatic events, and women remain a small minority in the European Parliament, but they could be interpreted as moves in the greater participation of women in political life. But at the popular level, 1979 tells a somewhat different story.

Figures for the differential participation of men and women in the first European election appear in Table IV.4. They show that men were generally more involved in the campaign than women: more interested in it, more often reached by it, and in every country except the Netherlands more likely to have voted at the

74

end of it. In some cases the sex differences were quite large. They were most evident for levels of campaign interest in Germany, Italy and Ireland, where differences amounted to 17 per cent, 16 per cent and 11 per cent respectively. German and Italian women were also much less exposed to the campaign than were their menfolk. On turn-out, however, the sex gap narrowed considerably in most countries (persisting substantially only in Germany, where a difference of 14 per cent remained), while in the Netherlands marginally more women than men went to the polls.

In general these findings, and the Eurobarometre predictions mentioned earlier, confirm traditional patterns in political research. It is part of the conventional wisdom of both national and comparative studies that women are less interested in politics, less involved and less likely to vote. But recent research suggests that there has been a reduction, in some countries at least, in differences in participation between the sexes. In France, for example, 31 per cent of women declared themselves 'interested in politics' in 1978 compared to 13 per cent in 1953, and over the same period the proportion saying that they were not at all interested fell from 60 per cent to 19.5 per cent. Though these figures still indicate differences in the levels of interest between the sexes (comparable figures for men were 49 per cent interested and 13 per cent not interested in 1978), the differences have declined since the 1950s (Charlot, 1980). British research tells a similar story. In fact the most recent surveys of general elections in Britain show that there are no significant differences between the sexes either in their interest in the campaign or in their propensity to vote (Sarlvik and Crewe, 1982). In the British case, then, it would appear that the European election may have re-opened differences in participation between the sexes which are less prevalent on the domestic political front at present. In the absence of similar data from elsewhere, we are unable to comment on how the participation levels of the sexes compared to national elections in the other countries of the Community. But we believe that such comparisons could prove interesting in the future.

Women's levels of interest and participation in politics are undoubtedly changing. To some extent these changes reflect structural factors peculiar to specific political systems. (The French figures cited above, for example, reflect the late enfranchisement of women in France in 1944). But they also reflect changing perceptions of the female role, new educational and work opportunities for women (cf. Blumler, McQuail and Nossiter, 1975 and 1976), and shifting definitions of politics which are common, though unevenly diffused, throughout the Community. In this light, it will be interesting to compare the findings reported here with the results of surveys conducted after future European elections.

Age

The influence of age on involvement in the European election was intriguingly open to two contrary sets of advance expectations. On the one hand, young people might have been specially responsive to the European message, first, because they were less committed than their elders to fixed patterns of domestic partisan alignments and issues (hence more 'free' to look outward to Europe), and second, because empirical research in the early 1970s (Inglehart, 1977) had disclosed a pattern among young people of stronger adherence to so-called 'post-material values', including a greater receptivity to supra-national identities. On the other hand, because political participation is a learned activity, which tends to be reinforced by increasing practice, we could expect rates of campaign involvement to be lowest among the youngest electors and to rise steadily with advancing age.

Much of the post-election survey evidence supports the latter thesis, though the influence of age does differ considerably according to the form of involvement being measured. On the whole, young Europeans, unless they were quite well-educated (a factor to which we turn in the next section) were rather unimpressed by the Community elections. Table IV.5 compares the interest levels, exposure rates and turn-out records of five age groups into which our respondents were divided. This shows that although young people received almost as much election material through the mass media and other channels as their elders, in a number of countries their interest tended to be below average, and they were decidedly less likely to have voted at the polls. It can be seen that in those countries where no sanctions against abstention were applicable, turn-out was typically lowest among 18-24 year olds, rose steadily to a peak at 55-64 years of age, then fell off somewhat among the elderly, due probably to a combination of factors: social isolation; physical inability to get to the polls; and higher proportions of women in the post-retirement age group. And the slope of higher voting participation with increasing age was particularly noticeable in the countries with a low turn-out - Britain and Denmark - and least evident in Germany.

The unwillingness of the young to turn out for Europe was yet more striking when viewed from two other angles. First, their relative failure to go to the polls in June 1979 was not merely a reflection of their tendency to abstain at any election. This can be seen from Table IV.6, which applies only to those sample members in five countries(4) who reported that they did vote in their country's previous general election, divides them by age, and shows in each age category how many individuals failed to vote at the European election. It can be seen that, except in the Netherlands, the youngest of these previous voters failed most often to cast ballots again in June 1979. And they were particularly likely to have ignored the European election in Britain and France.

Nor, secondly, was the lower turn-out of young voters a reflection of a weaker attachment to the European cause on their part. Table IV.7 shows the percentages of the respondents in the different age groups who maintained that Common Market membership was a 'good thing' for their country. By this criterion only in Denmark(5) were younger people clearly less supportive of the Community than their elders. Elsewhere their outlook on EEC membership was as positive as that of older people (or in a few cases only marginally less favourable). Three-way tables not presented here suggest that much youthful support for the Common Market stemmed from the influence of education: younger electoral cohorts were better educated, and better educated voters were more positively disposed to the Community. Even so, the overall failure of age to correlate with attitudes to the European Community, which Table IV.7 illustrates, stands in marked contrast to the powerful association of age with voting rates, which Table IV.5 depicts. Among younger citizens, at least, the impulses of a low-key direct election were too weak to convert their moderately pro-European sentiments into definite voting decisions.

Educational background
    There is nothing enigmatic about the role of education in orienting electors to the European campaign: education exerted a consistently cosmopolitan influence on electoral involvement. The evidence for this assertion appears in Table IV.8, which shows how educational background was associated with campaign interest and turn-out, separately for each of the five age categories into which our samples were divided. (The equivalent figures for campaign exposure have been omitted to avoid excessive tabular detail, but they disclose similar trends.) Three findings concerning the impact of education on campaign interest deserve attention. First, in

almost every case interest steadily increased with each increase in the respondents' school-leaving age. Second, the tendency for interest to rise as people aged, which appeared slight in the previous section when educational controls were not applied, became quite marked among the most highly educated sample members in most of the countries. Third, the impact of higher education was so powerful that in all countries, except France and Germany, the youngest age group, in general the least interested one, when well-educated, was more interested in the campaign than any of its minimally educated elders. The relationship of education to turn-out was similar - except that the above mentioned tendency for better educated youngsters to be more involved than their less educated seniors was reversed in every national sample but one (Denmark). Even well-educated European youth then, shared its generation's reluctance to go to the polls in June 1979.

Demographic summary

In essence, we have found that the electoral audience for the European campaign over-represented men, the middle-aged and the better educated. To some extent, women compensated for their lack of interest and attention by voting in quite respectable numbers on polling day. Young people, however, even when positively disposed to the Community, very often failed to vote. And the campaign was least successful of all in penetrating the minimally-educated young electors of Europe.

Partisan mobilisation

It is no easy matter to discern the influence of party preferences on voters' readiness to participate in the European election. Three problems are involved. First, demography confuses the issue. Insofar as political parties recruit support unevenly from different demographic sectors, we would expect inequalities of involvement due to such background factors to be confounded with differential partisan mobilisation. Socialist and other left-wing parties, for example, which depend more heavily on manual workers and younger electors, could experience greater difficulties of mobilisation due to the effects of education and age discussed in the previous section. Perhaps it should be emphasised, however, that this process is not always one way: there may be an interplay between demographic and partisan pressures. A striking example drawn from our 1979 evidence should suffice to illustrate the point. As we have seen, on average men tended to be more involved in the

European campaign than women. But among the supporters of a handful of party groups - all associated with the European Liberals and Democrats as it happened - women were more interested in the campaign than men; and in the case of the French Parti Republicain they actually showed a greater propensity to vote by a clear margin of 12 per cent. So exceptional was this result that it is difficult not to ascribe the greater involvement of these women to the influence of the distinguished leader of the UDF list, Simone Veil.

A second problem is one of sheer presentation, owing to the national distinctness of each country's party system, as well as the multiplicity of parties that compete for votes in some states. Our wish is to present the cross-national evidence in as clearly comparative a form as possible without obscuring the individuality of the national systems. We have therefore chosen to present our data in a table based on the European party blocs (how the parties are grouped in the Parliament itself), while confining our attention to the major parties of each country.

A third problem concerns the choice of benchmark for measuring differential campaign involvement and turn-out by partisanship at the European election. Based on comparisons of voting support at the European election with votes cast at the most recent general election in each country, Inglehart and Rabier (1979) concluded that, '... the so-called 'swing to the right' (was) anything but evident'. But there are severe limitations to this form of comparison. First, the periods between the two elections varied greatly across the different Community countries, ranging from one week in the Italian case to three years for Germany. Inter-party swings in one country are hardly comparable with those in another when the corresponding time spans are so divergent. Second, factors other than a party's ability to generate support at the European election could have played on such inter-election swings. The biggest electoral trend against a party found anywhere in the Community occurred in Ireland, when Fianna Fail's share of the poll was 16 per cent lower than in 1977. But most commentators agree that this decline owed more to the industrial and energy crises suffered between the two elections than to campaign factors and events. Third, share-of-poll percentages can give a misleading picture of the mobilisation of party groups, if overall turn-out levels differed greatly between the two elections, as was the case in many countries. In Britain, for example, the share-of-poll comparison shows a decline in Labour voting from 37 per cent to 32 per cent and an increase in Conservative voting from 44 per cent to 48 per cent. But in reality this Conservative increase was achieved with half as many votes as had been obtained at the general election one month earlier. Although the share-of-poll figures do give a comparative indication of the fortunes of competing parties at the two elections, they provide no indication of the parties' abilities to bring out their available support at the time of the European campaign.

In order to eliminate the influence of varying time scales, and to minimise the impact of shifts in party allegiances that may have preceded the European election, we have focused our analysis on groups of party supporters defined by their current voting intentions in a prospective national election, had one been held in June 1979. By this criterion, differential partisan mobilisation occurred when a body of individuals saying they would vote for a given party at a domestic election (say, Labour) were more or less involved in the European campaign than those identifying with a different party (say, the Conservatives).

The mobilisation performance of the main parties of Europe - as indexed by the interest levels, campaign exposure rates and turn-out records of their supporters - can be readily compared by glancing at the three relevant sections of Table IV.9. Two overall impressions strongly emerge from this material. First, Europe's general election 'don't knows' (the figures for whom appear in the extreme right-hand column of the table) also took exceedingly little notice of the European election. In every country, by each criterion, they were less galvanised by the campaign (often by big margins) than was the least involved band of partisans. For turn-out especially, this 'participation deficit' widened enormously everywhere. Second, supporters of Socialist and Social Democratic Parties were almost invariably less involved in the campaigns than were adherents of parties to their left and, more importantly, of their main centre and right-of-centre rivals. Only in Italy did the Socialists consistently manage to do as well as the other main parties in these terms. Elsewhere Socialist voters were less interested in the campaign than all other party-support groups. It is true that the French Socialists followed the campaign more heavily than did right-wing voters, but the tendency for consumption of election messages to increase as voters become more left-wing is a firmly-rooted feature of the French political communication system (Blumler, Cayrol and Thoveron, 1978). And again, in turn-out, Socialists abstained more often than did the supporters of

80

any other party in every country (with only a very marginal exception in the case of the Danish Progressives).

It should be emphasised that this pattern was not due to any overall weakness of support for the Socialist parties of Europe at that time. On the contrary, in response to the question about current voting intent, the Socialist parties obtained larger shares of support than they had won at the ballot box in the previous general election. Differential turn-out, therefore, rather than a swing away from Socialist parties, explains the European election result. Developments in Ireland well illustrate the value of this kind of analysis. Ireland was one of two countries where the main Socialist Party obtained a higher proportion of the poll at the European election than in the previous general election.(6) Yet our survey shows that the European election voting rates were lower among supporters of the Irish Labour Party than among adherents of Fianna Fail or Fine Gael. This was not due to any unrepresent- ativeness of the Irish post-election survey, which matched the actual national result well (e.g. giving Labour a 16 per cent share of the poll compared to the true result of 14.5 per cent). In effect, what our analysis shows is that the Irish Labour Party could have done better. It had reserves of support which were not mobilised. In common with most of the rest of Europe, its rivals were better able to activate their supporters.

It is true that the under-mobilisation of Socialists partly reflects their demographic origins. But that is not the whole story. When educational controls are applied to the partisan voting intent groups, such that one can analyse differences in educational levels within parties and differences between parties at the same educa- tional level, the following trends emerge:

i) The better educated Socialists were generally more interested in the campaign and more exposed to it than were their less educated comrades - and particularly more likely to vote in Britain, Denmark and Ireland.

ii) With few exceptions, the better educated Socialists were less interested, less exposed to the campaign and less likely to vote than those of their educational peers who backed other parties.

iii) Similarly, the minimally educated Socialists were usually less involved in the European campaign than were supporters of the other major parties in almost every country (with exceptions only for turn-out in Germany and for campaign exposure in Belgium, Denmark and France).

It is tempting to see in these patterns the influence of an ideological incompatibility between the ideals of Europeanism and traditional Socialist preoccupations with equality and social class. However, such a strain did not inhibit the mobilisation of their support by the more disciplined parties to the left of the Socialists, whether their view of the Community was largely critical, as in the case of the French Communists and the predominantly left-organised People's Movement Against the Common Market in Denmark, or more favourable, as in the case of the Italian Communist Party.

A bifurcated electorate?

As a force for reaching voters who, by disposition or situation, could have been initially less aware, the first direct election of the European Parliament emerges from the above analysis with mixed marks. Opponents of the European Community did not comprehensively ignore the campaign (except in Britain where, admittedly, they were numerically strong), though they often stayed at home on polling day. At the opinion level, however, lack of conviction that the Community Parliament could be an effective and relevant political force posed a more stubborn obstacle to diffusion of the campaign's appeal. Otherwise, Socialists often behaved as if ambivalent about participation in European electoral politics. On some counts women were less fully engaged by the campaign than men, but they somewhat redressed the balance on polling day itself. Younger and less educated citizens (particularly when these traits were combined) were singularly indifferent to the election.

Such a mixed result also emerges if we divide the samples by yet another criterion - level of interest in the campaign - and then see how the groups so formed reacted to the election in other respects. In Table IV.10 we compare those respondents who said they had been 'very' or 'quite' interested in the European election campaign with those who were only a 'little' or 'not at all' interested on three quite revealing measures: frequency of exposure to the television campaign; impressions of the Parliament's likely future impact; and turn-out at the polls.

The first two bases of comparison convey the impression of a European electorate that was sharply divided in 1979 into two distinct layers - an involved and aware minority and a more indifferent majority. Typically, half the former followed the campaign more or less daily compared with only a tenth to a quarter of the latter. Typically, large majorities of the interested voters expected decisions of the European Parliament to have a significant effect on people's lives in the future compared with only minorities of the uninterested ones. But although those individuals who were uninterested in the campaign were also less likely to have voted on polling day, in this crucial respect the differences between the two 'layers' noticeably narrowed. Indeed, bearing in mind the much larger percentages of the samples who rated themselves no more than a little interested in the campaign, these less interested voters constituted major portions of the poll in all the Community countries.

NOTES

1. Post-election surveys invariably over-estimate electoral turn-out; that is, the proportions claiming to have voted in the election exceed official turn-out statistics. Comparisons of official and survey turn-out figures for each of the eight countries appear below (the survey calculations excluded 'refusal' and 'don't know' replies from the percentage base):

	Official turn-out %	Post-election survey %
Belgium	91	91
Denmark	48	57
France	61	78
Germany	63	73
Great Britain	32	43
Ireland	64	73
Italy	86	94
Netherlands	58	66

Explanations of this phenomenon sometimes allege deception on the part of those interviewed. Voting may be seen as a citizen's duty and respondents may claim to have fulfilled their obligations when in some cases they have not done so. But, though there may be some plausibility in this view, it is unlikely to provide a complete explanation. Part of the difference can be accounted for by inaccuracies in electoral registers; insofar as these include electors who have died, moved house or emigrated, they are likely to over-estimate the electorate actually available for voting. But a great part of the differences can be explained in terms of the survey's difficulties in reaching non-voters. Non-voters fall into two groups: those unable to vote for one reason or another, and those unwilling to do so. Both groups, though particularly the latter, are likely to be under-represented in a survey conducted immediately after an election. At any given time some people will be sick, perhaps hospitalised, away on business, on holiday, or engaged in some other activity which will have prevented them from taking part in an election; some of these activities will have also precluded their participation in an electoral survey. Similarly, those who have chosen not to vote are unlikely to feel motivated to take part in an interview about the election. In other words, the survey tends to be more available, and, more importantly, more acceptable to people who have been able and willing to vote than to those who have not. In short, the official turn-out statistics are calculated on a base which includes all technically eligible electors, whereas the survey turn-out is calculated on the basis of those who first agreed to take part in the interview at all, and, secondly, agreed to answer the question on voting. The differences between the two turn-out figures can therefore be accounted for in terms of an under-representation of non-voters through non-participation in the survey, rather than an over-representation of voters through deception. This may have some implications for the findings reported here. Insofar as the survey may under-represent the more apathetic non-voter, our findings may slightly over-estimate levels of interest and commitment to be found in the electorate and may also under-estimate differences between the more and less active demographic and political groups.

2. Non-voters were asked (in every country except Belgium) to say why they had not voted. In most countries the largest category of replies covered 'personal reasons', i.e. sickness, holidays, business commitments and so on, followed by a lack of interest in European elections, Parliament or European affairs in general. Around 10 per cent of non-voters in Denmark and Britain also mentioned hostility to or disapproval of European institutions as a reason for not voting, but in other countries the figure was much lower. But there

are interesting differences in the reasons offered by those adopting contrasting opinions on their country's membership of the Community. In some countries reliable comment is precluded by the size of the anti-membership non-voting group; but the following comparisons are worth noting:

	Denmark		France		G.B.		Ireland		Netherlds	
	pro	anti	pro	anti	pro	anti	pro	anti	pro	anti
Reasons for not voting:					Percentages					
Personal	31	28	44	28	36	14	37	21	22	5
Lack of interest in EC affairs	15	11	9	24	13	29	10	29	10	22
Hostility to EC institutions, ties with EC	6	18	2	8	1	18	-	6	2	32
Other reasons	48	43	45	40	60	39	53	44	66	41
Total N =	134	96	85	25	124	265	111	66	146	37

In most countries, those adopting pro-European positions on Community membership were far more likely to offer personal reasons for not voting than were those who opposed their country's membership, whereas the latter were more likely to offer the 'Europeanness' of the election as a reason for not having participated in it.

3. Results of the IIC project's content analysis of election programmes on television point to France as one of the two Community countries whose campaigns stood out for extent of preoccupation with domestic rather than European themes (the other was Ireland).

4. Data about previous general election voting were not obtained in the German survey.

5. The Danish pattern reflects the above-average support of young electors in that country for left-wing parties, which were also strongly anti-Market in outlook.

6. The other country was Italy.

Table IV.1   Evaluations of Community membership and involvement in the European election

	Very or quite interested in the campaign							
	Percentages							
	B	Dk	F	G	GB	Irl	I	NI
Membership of the EC is:								
A good thing	34	48	46	59	53	45	34	52
Neither good nor bad	22	25	38	27	21	15	22	27
A bad thing	32	47	38	31	15	27	32	29
Don't know	5	25	27	-	18	8	1	13

	Mean number of channels of exposure							
	B	Dk	F	G	GB	Irl	I	NI
A good thing	2.7	3.1	2.8	4.2	3.0	3.1	4.7	2.7
Neither good nor bad	1.9	2.2	2.3	2.8	1.8	2.4	3.9	1.5
A bad thing	2.4	3.5	2.9	2.8	1.7	2.6	4.9	2.8
Don't know	0.9	1.9	1.8	-	1.5	1.9	1.7	0.9

	Turn-out: Per cent voting[a]					
	Dk	F	G	GB	Irl	NI
A good thing	59	81	85	64	79	76
Neither good nor bad	36	75	62	35	66	71
A bad thing	58	62	66	27	62	49
Don't know	34	52	-	33	52	50

a   Belgium and Italy omitted from all turn-out tables of this chapter due to 'compulsory' voting.

Table IV.2   Assessments of relevance of European Parliament and involvement in the European election campaign

		Very or quite interested in the campaign						
				Percentages				
	B	Dk	F	G	GB	Irl	I	Nl
EP will have:								
Great effect	51	63	58	76	47	58	53	52
Some effect	49	45	48	69	37	39	35	54
Not much	34	35	35	35	23	26	22	38
None	10	28	25	19	14	16		25
Don't know	6	24	30	-	15	16	10	16

		Mean number of channels of exposure						
	B	Dk	F	G	GB	Irl	I	Nl
Great effect	3.3	3.8	3.5	4.4	2.9	3.4	5.8	2.6
Some effect	3.1	3.3	2.7	4.1	2.4	3.0	4.8	2.5
Not much	2.4	2.8	2.6	3.4	2.0	2.6	4.1	2.2
None	1.8	2.1	2.1	2.8	1.5	2.3		2.0
Don't know	1.0	1.9	1.8	-	1.3	1.7	2.5	0.9

	Turn-out: Per cent voting					
	Dk	F	G	GB	Irl	Nl
Great effect	64	86	85	56	79	70
Some effect	55	81	87	48	75	80
Not much	51	79	73	37	73	70
None	40	69	59	29	61	57
Don't know	38	62	-	27	55	49

Table IV.3 Combined attitudes to the Community and Parliament by campaign involvement

	Very or quite interested							
	Percentages							
Effect of EP[a]	Belgium		Denmark		France		Italy	
	+	-	+	-	+	-	+	-
Membership of the EC is:								
A good thing	53	52	52	41	55	46	41	25
Neither good nor bad	43	15	40	17	46	27	30	16
A bad thing	43	-	58	42	52	30	40	29

	Mean number of channels of exposure							
Effect of EP	Belgium		Denamrk		France		Italy	
	+	-	+	-	+	-	+	-
Membership of the EC is:								
A good thing	3.2	2.5	3.4	2.7	3.1	2.5	5.1	4.3
Neither good not bad	2.8	1.8	2.6	2.3	2.5	2.4	4.5	3.6
A bad thing	4.7	1.7	4.3	2.9	3.8	2.5	5.3	4.9

a + A great effect or some effect
   - Not much effect or none at all

88

Table IV.4   Involvement in the election by sex

	Per cent very or quite interested		Mean no. of channels		Turn-out: Per cent voting	
	M	F	M	F	M	F
Belgium	30	23	2.3	2.0	–	–
Denmark	44	36	3.1	2.6	53	48
France	43	37	3.0	2.4	78	75
Germany	56	39	4.1	3.3	76	62
Great Britain	33	28	2.5	1.9	46	39
Ireland	38	27	2.9	2.5	71	68
Italy	38	22	5.1	3.6	–	–
Netherlands	40	32	2.3	1.7	64	68

Table IV.5   Involvement in the election by age

| | | Very or quite interested | | |
Age	18-24	25-34	35-54	55-64	65+
		Percentages			
Belgium	24	29	24	30	28
Denmark	36	41	36	43	44
France	30	36	38	49	49
Germany	44	57	46	43	44
Great Britain	26	25	30	39	35
Ireland	26	34	37	33	27
Italy	26	29	30	32	30
Netherlands	39	35	36	39	34
		Mean number of channels			
Age	18-24	25-34	35-54	55-64	65+
Belgium	2.2	2.2	2.1	2.0	2.1
Denmark	3.1	3.2	2.7	2.7	2.5
France	2.7	2.6	2.5	2.6	2.5
Germany	3.8	4.8	3.6	3.5	3.3
Great Britain	1.9	2.2	2.2	2.3	2.2
Ireland	2.6	2.7	2.7	2.8	2.4
Italy	4.7	4.5	4.4	3.9	3.8
Netherlands	2.3	2.3	2.0	1.9	1.6
		Turn-out: Per cent voting			
Age	18-24	25-34	35-54	55-64	65+
Denmark	39	49	55	51	53
France	63	72	78	83	85
Germany	61	71	74	70	62
Great Britain	27	36	40	58	54
Ireland	55	67	74	75	72
Netherlands	62	62	67	71	72

Table IV.6   Abstention at the European election among previous general election voters
by age

Percentages

Age	Britain	Denmark	France	Ireland	Netherlands
18-24	65	51	35	26	19
25-34	57	47	25	20	25
35-54	55	40	19	15	20
55-64	38	40	16	14	16
65+	39	41	13	17	15

Table IV.7   Support for membership of the European Community by age

Age	Per cent supporting EC membership				
	18-24	25-34	35-54	55-64	65+
Belgium	59	51	50	54	18
Denmark	19	35	42	41	46
France	49	48	46	56	54
Germany	69	69	58	52	51
Great Britain	35	40	35	44	37
Ireland	57	55	58	55	52
Italy	76	74	79	69	68
Netherlands	47	53	53	59	45

91

Table IV.8   The impact of the campaign on age and education sub-groups

Age	School-leaving age	18-24	Very or quite interested 25-34	35-54	55-64	65+
Belgium	-15	6	24	12	20	22
	16-17	13	33	33	30	17
	18+	32	29	33	54	59
Denmark	-15	29	29	33	40	43
	16-17	29	35	25	50	44
	18+	46	55	54	63	62
France	-15	a	34	34	45	49
	16-17	25	39	37	64	45
	18+	31	34	45	53	56
Germany	-15	32	52	41	38	37
	16-17	57	55	42	41	56
	18+	44	65	65	62	65
Great Britain	-15	12	20	25	31	29
	16-17	22	18	27	59	62
	18+	47	48	45	62	67
Ireland	-15	27	28	30	22	19
	16-17	16	29	36	40	46
	18+	35	45	50	54	37
Italy	-15	10	26	24	29	26
	16-17	28	33	40	-	-
	18+	32	33	51	60	83
Netherlands	-15	21	19	27	28	30
	16-17	24	34	44	54	47
	18+	48	45	42	57	38

92

Table IV.8   (Continued)

Age		18-24	Turn-out: Per cent voting			65+
			25-34	35-54	55-64	
	School-leaving age					
Denmark	-15	27	42	56	53	60
	16-17	33	47	58	73	62
	18+	62	73	70	80	82
France	-15	a	69	78	84	87
	16-17	59	72	76	93	73
	18+	67	75	80	76	92
Germany	-15	64	74	70	65	56
	16-17	77	60	73	76	75
	18+	52	70	83	83	80
Great Britain	-15	17	28	38	57	50
	16-17	22	36	38	62	81
	18+	44	53	51	86	75
Ireland	-15	64	69	75	78	72
	16-17	54	73	81	86	74
	18+	58	72	75	87	79
Netherlands	-15	43	62	64	69	72
	16-17	63	61	70	71	82
	18+	66	62	69	79	67

a   Too few cases for analysis.

Table IV.9   Partisan differences of mobilisation effectiveness

	Left	Comm.	Per cent very or quite interested Demo-cratic Socs.	Libs.	Pro-gress Dems.	Cons/Christian Dems.	Other	Don't know (No vote intent)
Belgium			23	34		33	36a	11
Denmark	60b		33	53	37	46c		29
France		49	39	49d	48			15
Germany			49	59		55		10
Great Britain			25	34		39		19
Ireland			30		32	39		25
Italy		34	34			29		11
Netherlands			30	51		36	57c	23

Mean number of channels of exposure

	Left	Comm.	Democratic Socs.	Libs.	Progress Dems.	Cons/Christian Dems.	Other	Don't know
Belgium			2.1	2.6		2.5	3.2a	1.5
Denmark	4.5b		2.6	3.1	2.5	3.2c		2.1
France		3.2	2.7	2.5	2.4			1.8
Germany			3.7	4.4		3.8		2.7
Great Britain			1.9	2.2		2.6		1.5
Ireland			2.5		2.9	2.8		2.2
Italy		4.8	4.7			4.4		3.5
Netherlands			1.9	2.4		1.9	2.8e	1.3

Turn-out: Per cent voting

	Left	Comm.	Democratic Socs.	Libs.	Progress Dems.	Cons/Christian Dems.	Other	Don't know
Denmark	72b		49	68	46	66c		32
France		85	76	81d	84			28
Germany			75	83		79		22
Great Britain			38	40		52		24
Ireland			72		83	80		40
Netherlands			67	76		76	79e	22

a   Belgian linguistic parties, VU, FDF, RW, PRLW, VLAAMS BLOCK
b   Left Socialists and socialist People's Party
c   Conservative and Centre Democrats
d   UDF
e   D66

Table IV.10   Selected comparisons of interested (+) and uninterested (-) electors

	B		Dk		F		G		GB		Irl		I		NI	
	+	-	+	-	+	-	+	-	+	-	+	-	+	-	+	-
Per cent followed TV campaign nearly daily or daily	44	10	58	19	49	15	50	24	41	18	52	13	48	14	49	14
Per cent saying Parliament will have great or some effect	54	21	60	38	58	36	64	24	70	44	70	41	73	49	46	23
Per cent turn-out			68	40	89	68	88	52	77	27	85	65			84	58

V THE PROCESS OF ELECTION INVOLVEMENT

In this chapter we try to bring together into a more ordered perspective many of the influences on popular responses to the European election, which we have so far considered separately. Although this attempt is (necessarily) speculative and a matter of personal interpretation, all the conclusions reached are supported by quite clear patterns of empirical evidence.

From the findings of the previous chapter, readers might have concluded that involvement in the 1979 campaign resembled a river fed by many diverse tributaries: it flowed, as it were, from the sexes, ages and educational backgrounds of voters, their party allegiances, and their attitudes to the European Community, including their views on its Parliament's prospects of exerting effective power in the future. For three reasons, however, we were unwilling to leave it at that.

First, there was a problem of overlapping factors to face and disentangle. We have met this type of difficulty earlier at several points - for instance, in the association of age with education, both of which were related in turn to interest in the campaign and turn-out. Another example is the seeming dependence of turn-out on both a higher education and a pro-European opinion. Were these separately distinguishable influences on voting behaviour? Or did they merely stand in for each other (better educated people also being more positively disposed to the EEC)? We cannot tell by considering them in isolation. And the problem becomes yet more acute as the web of potentially interrelated variables expands. Fortunately, a number of statistical tools for sorting out such relationships are available, out of which we have adopted the technique of regression analysis. This is designed to estimate the independent power of a given factor (say, a pro-European outlook) to explain variation on another factor (say, turn-out) while all other measured influences are being held constant.

Second, we had to face the issue of the sequence in which such influences made themselves felt, and to arrange these data systematically. In what manner might people's demographic traits, orientations to Europe, interest in and exposure to the campaign have been related to each other and to major election outcomes? We could have tackled such a question by simply taking some criterion of involvement, such as voting on polling day, and seeing how far each of its apparent correlates was independently associated with it when tested by regression analysis. But such an approach would have done violence to the very nature of election involvement, which is not an abrupt event but the emergent product of a train of interconnected processes. We therefore decided to fashion as convincing a model as we could conceive of those interacting involvement processes that might have been operative during the European campaign. It would have an empirical foundation, for in developing it we would be guided by the cross-tabular evidence about the separate concomitants of involvement with which we were already familiar. But the relationships postulated in it would be tested through a series of regression analyses designed to confirm or deny their presence when multi-variate controls were applied.

This aspiration was admittedly in some conflict with the static nature of our data base. Teasing 'processes' out of such material is like converting a still photograph into a moving picture. Our justification for the attempt is two-fold. It ensures that the evidence is used, not in the spirit of a random fishing expedition, but in pursuit of systematic insights into the sources of European election participation. Inferences are involved, but readers can judge their plausibility for themselves. In addition, such a procedure exploits the cross-national comparability of our evidence, enabling us to see how well the proposed model reflects the election responses of each of our national samples. We believe that the results of this approach do convey a convincing picture of the dynamics of public involvement in the first European election, doing justice both to forces that played on the process throughout the Community at large, and to those that were singularly operative in certain individual campaigns.

Third, there was the question of communication impact to face and answer. Was there any credible evidence of mass media influence on how voters had participated in the 1979 election and on the impressions they formed of European issues at the time? In previous chapters we have plotted the distributions of campaign interest and exposure across national publics and electoral sub-groups. But we still do not know whether such communication factors mattered at all to the main outcomes of the first Community election. Table V.1 suggests that campaign variables were quite powerfully associated with the readiness of electors to go to the polls in June 1979. In all six countries where no official obligation exerted pressure on citizens to cast ballots, those individuals who were more interested in the campaign, and those who had followed it in a larger number of media channels, evidently were more likely to have voted - and by quite sizeable margins in some states. But strong as they appear, such bivariate relationships cannot be taken at face value and must be examined in the context of controls for potentially confounding influences.

In fact, two end-results of the election were open, through regression analysis, to a cumulative exploration that might assign some place to communication variables: people's awareness of the election issues, which we decided to measure by the total number of issues mentioned by sample members as having emerged from the campaign; and turn-out, or whether they had voted or abstained on polling day. In seeking evidence of the impact of communi-cation on such consequences, we were again limited by the cross-sectional character of the data. For the purpose of these analyses, we inferred an 'effect' of a communication variable when it was still associated with an election outcome after all other measured influences had been taken into account. In principle, such an inference is open to challenge on two grounds. For one thing, reverse causation could apply. Such an interpretation would be highly implausible in this case, however, where we are dealing with such truly terminal outcomes of the election process as issue awareness, which probably was hazy at best for many individuals at the outset of the campaign (and so could only have been built up during it) and voting at the polls, which actually took place at the end of the campaign. More seriously, the evidence of an effect could be spurious, reflecting the simultaneous impact on both communication and outcome variables of yet other 'third' variables. Though such an explanation can never be entirely ruled out, its force can be diminished by introducing into the equation (as we have tried to do) as many variables that could have functioned in this way as possible. Indeed, we consider that the analyses presented below do pinpoint some important effects of exposure to election materials during the 1979 campaign that were unlikely to have been due to other causes.(1)

A model of European election involvement

Our model of how key forces could have encouraged popular involvement in the European election is displayed diagramatically in Figure V.1. The processes depicted there reflect two major organising principles. One is that a more positive attitude to Europe would have engendered a keener interest in the campaign, which in turn would have generated more exposure to election communication, leading on to issue learning and thence to turn-out. The other is that the seeds of a positive European awareness were ultimately rooted in people's demographic characteristics and partisan affiliations. In addition, a place in the model has been found, alongside campaign exposure, for viewers' positive and negative evaluations of the television campaign to have affected issue learning and voting rates. Moreover, by positioning the variable of issue awareness before that of turn-out, an assumption of 'agenda-setting' theory (Weaver, et al., 1981) has been incorporated - namely, that the actual performance of voting is conditional on the citizen having formed a focused impression of the issues at stake. But the lynch-pin of the model is the premise that positive attitudes to Europe were a precursor of high campaign involvement. This is not to prejudge the issue of whether the direct election was in this sense a truly European affair but rather to open it, hopefully, to fruitful examination. The regression analyses should then show a) how far and in what countries popular involvement had actually developed along such a 'European route' and b), insofar as it followed other paths, which 'non-European' factors had noticeably promoted electoral participation.

To be tested, then, the model required a sequence of five successive regression analyses - at the stages signposted by Roman numerals at the bottom of the Figure - each one to include, as would-be predictors, all variables to the left of the Roman numeral concerned. Thus, all variables of demographic circumstances and party preference (measured by how sample members would have voted at a domestic general election) would first be regressed on ratings of the likely effectiveness of future actions by the European Parliament on people's lives. This latter variable was chosen to represent 'European outlook' at this point (for all samples except the British one, where evaluation of Common Market membership was used instead), because, as we saw in the previous chapter, among the measures of European opinion available to us, it was the strongest predictor of voters' levels of campaign participation. Then the demographic, party and European outlook measures would be regressed on campaign interest - and so on until all the variables included in the Figure would be regressed penultimately on issue awareness and finally on turn-out.

We do not claim that such a model can do full justice to the complexity of the relationships involved or that certain elements could not have been plausibly rearranged. Nevertheless, the processes outlined in Figure V.1 do seem to make the best preliminary sense of the available evidence. The most serious limitation of the model is its portrayal of all influence relationships as linear and one way, whereas in reality some were very likely reciprocal and mutually cumulative. Yet the case for approaching the data along the proposed lines stands up well to scrutiny when particular instances of such relationships are considered in detail. A case in point is the probable close connection between the amount of interest that people took in the campaign and the extent of their exposure to it in the mass media and elsewhere. Whereas the model treats the former as prior to the latter, the process could have been reversed with exposure to election materials whetting voters' appetites to seek out yet more of the same.(2) Nevertheless, in the case of a campaign which typically provoked more electoral dissatisfaction than praise, the assumption that interest would grow as more campaign messages were consumed seemed less well-founded than the opposite expectation that as interest rose the campaign would be followed more eagerly. After all, the notion of 'election overkill' reflects a very real fear that at some point too much exposure will depress interest. Yet again, people's views about the likely effectiveness of the European Parliament could have been treated as a third outcome of the election, instead of as a source of campaign interest and exposure (as in Figure V.1). But the early place assigned this variable in the model at least has the merit of imposing a demanding test of the impact of campaign factors on the other election outcomes of issue learning and turn-out. For it means that exposure to the campaign (say) will surface from the regression analyses as an influence on voting (say) only after all of its association with people's impressions of the Parliament's future impact has been controlled for and discounted. In this way we are even running the risk of artificially depressing our estimates of campaign effects instead of inflating them.

But how did the model fare when the regression analyses were performed? These were carried out separately for each of the eight national samples (omitting turn-out from the Belgian and Italian analyses because almost everyone had voted in those countries). The resulting data are rich, and a procedure for coherently unfolding them is required. To familiarise readers with what can emerge from such an analysis for a single country, we start by showing in Figure V.2 the significant paths between variables that appeared in the regressions from the British data set. A path was never included unless the relationship between the two connected variables was statistically significant at the P = .05 level, which means that it would have arisen by chance on only five out of 100 occasions. The numbers on the paths are beta weights, which in magnitude resemble correlation coefficients adjusted for the role of all other factors in the analysis and serve to index the strength of the relationship involved.(3) Similar diagrams laying out the regression results for all the other countries can be found in Appendix B. Next we present in Figure V.3 a revised version of the model, which, taking account of all the national results, best represents the involvement process as it worked itself out in the Community as a whole. This has been prepared by inscribing as solid arrows in the diagram all those paths that emerged as significant from at least five of the eight national analyses. Thereafter, we single out those countries where the results markedly diverged in some important way from the Community pattern, drawing on what we know about their campaigns to explain the deviations. Then we apply what we have learned to the two-sided 'enigma' of European election turn-out. Why, in all the countries where voting was unconstrained by some sanction, did voting rates fall well below those of the usual general election standard? And why, despite all the difficulties of staging an arousing campaign, did so many Europeans bother nevertheless to vote in June 1979? All this will have remained, however, at a micro level of analysis, concerned with those differences between individual voters that our survey data have allowed us to trace. And so, in a final section, we move briefly to a few questions that can be raised at a macro level of cross-national systems analysis. Why did turn-out rates differ among the member states in ways that previous general election voting behaviour would not have predicted? And to what extent might such differences have been due to different levels of campaign activity and media coverage obtaining in the various EEC countries?

The process of election involvement in Britain

Turning first to the British results, as displayed in Figure V.2 these highlight seven main trends:

i)   Positive evaluations of the Common Market were a prime predictor of British interest in the campaign, shaping this more emphatically than did any other variable in the model.   But campaign interest was also independently heightened by certain partisan preferences (notably Conservative allegiances), a better education and greater age.

ii)   The British were more likely to hold pro-European attitudes if they supported the Conservative Party, had stayed at school longer, and (to a lesser extent) were males.

iii)   Campaign interest powerfully regulated the exposure of British electors to European campaign communications, predicting their consumption of such materials far more effectively than did any other variable in the analysis.   However, male and better-educated electors followed the campaign more regularly as well.

iv)   British turn-out on polling day heavily depended on people's prior levels of campaign interest, the .37 beta weight for this association being higher than all but one of the other bivariate relations in the data (that between interest and exposure).   But older people and supporters of the Common Market were also more likely to have gone to the polls.

v)   Despite the significant impact of campaign interest on voting rates, heavier exposure to campaign communications was also an independent concomitant of higher turn-out.

vi)   Like turn-out, issue awareness was also a product of campaign influences - interest, exposure and positive evaluations of the TV coverage having all been independently related to this outcome.   But the demographic factors of education, age and sex (being male) predicted issue learning as well.

vii)   Although the path from issue awareness to turn-out was just statistically significant, its independent contribution to voting was in fact only slight.

Overall, the British data fit the original model quite well - except perhaps for the rather weak link between issue awareness and turn-out. The closeness of fit is illustrated by the relatively high multiple correlation coefficient of .57 that was obtained for the combined association with turn-out of all the variables included in the analysis. Accounting for as much as 32.5 per cent of all variation between those individuals who voted and those who abstained, this is an impressive level of explanation for a limited number of factors taken from such an economically designed survey to have achieved.

We concluded that the involvement process in Britain was firmly channelled along predominantly European grooves. Supporters of the Common Market, stemming disproportionately from Conservative and well-educated sectors of the population, were far more interested in the campaign and (partly because of that) more inclined to vote than were antagonistic, ambivalent and indifferent electors. Even party preference as such exerted no <u>independent</u> influence on voting participation. This is not to deny that partisans went to the polls in greater numbers than uncommitted electors. But party affiliation affected voting only insofar as the individuals concerned were more European-minded and more interested in the campaign. These results help to explain the exceptionally low British turn-out of June 1979, for at that time only a minority took a favourable view of Community membership, and at best most of the voters were only a 'little' interested in the election campaign. Among those extra paths shown in Figure V.2 which had not originally been included in the simplified model, some were in line with past studies of demographic constraints on political participation - such as the more dutiful approach to voting of older people and the greater ability of the better educated to tune in to election issues. Other paths, as already noted, reflected marked features of the British campaign - particularly the above-average participation of the Tory and pro-European elements of the public.

Election involvement processes: the Community at large

Figure V.3 provides an overview of the forces that apparently spurred popular involvement in the 1979 election in the Community as a whole. As previously explained, its paths identify those relationships that were statistically significant in at least a majority of the national samples. Before considering the results in detail, it may be useful to indicate for each individual country how far <u>all</u> the variables included in the analysis succeeded in predict-

103

ing the election outcomes with which we were concerned. This is shown by the following multiple correlation coefficients with turn-out in six samples and with issue awareness for Belgium and Italy:

Britain	-	.57
Germany	-	.55
Ireland	-	.50
Belgium	-	.49
Italy	-	.48
Denmark	-	.47
Holland	-	.44
France	-	.34

Thus, the model variables were most 'successful' in toto in accounting for turn-out in Britain and least 'successful' for France. In most cases, however, they explained about one-quarter of the variation between those who voted and those who stayed at home on polling day.

Within this overall pattern, six main features of the election involvement process in the community at large emerge from the results summarised in Figure V.3.

First, positive attitudes to Community affairs did pull their weight during the election. In most countries they were not directly associated with turn-out at the polls. They operated instead at an 'earlier' stage of the involvement process, serving as a funnel for campaign interest and through that indirectly contributing to the main election outcomes as well. Indeed, respondents' impressions of the likely impact of the elected Parliament's decisions on the lives of people like themselves were universally a more powerful source of their interest in the campaign than was any other measured variable. The model was less successful, however, in identifying the chief background sources of such an attitude. It is true that the better-educated voters were often more impressed with the likely relevance of the Parliament to people's lives in the future - as were supporters of one or more political party - in all the countries. But the relationships involved were usually quite modest and accounted overall for rather low percentages of the total amount of variance in attitudes to the Parliament. To all this, Britain was something of a national deviant in two respects. Pro-Market opinions featured more prominently there, a) because they impinged directly as well as indirectly on turn-out, and b) because the background variables explained far more of the variance in such attitudes than they did elsewhere.(4)

Second, party loyalties as such also pulled their weight during the 1979 campaigns. In five of the six countries where turn-out variance could be studied, European election voting was directly dependent on people's partisan affiliations as expressed by their general election voting intentions - the beta weights involved proving quite high in Germany and Ireland especially. This finding apparently confirms the importance for European turn-out of the process termed 'political mobilisation' by Inglehart and Rabier (1979), reflecting the efforts of certain parties and their more keen supporters to surpass their leading rivals at the polls. Yet such mobilisation may have facilitated other forms of involvement as well, most noticeably by heightening levels of public interest in the campaign. Whereas having a party preference often prompted voting, however, it only rarely favoured the cultivation of issue perceptions. In this sphere, the British sample was again an exception, having thrown up no direct path from any form of party preference to voting. This is not to deny that British partisans went to the polls in greater numbers than the uncommitted electors. But party affiliation affected voting there only insofar as the individuals concerned were more European-minded and more interested in the campaign.

Third, educational background was a powerful underlying force in the involvement process. In every country without exception, it fed all the intervening factors through which the campaign encouraged voting participation - outlook on Europe, campaign interest and campaign exposure. Playing no direct part in stimulating turn-out, then, a higher education was nevertheless often associated with a greater awareness of the election issues. The contrast with the previously noted role of partisanship is intriguing. Both factors independently impinged on all the variables that helped to build up a sense of involvement, but so far as the final election outcomes were concerned, party preference played on turn-out rather than issue awareness, and educational level influenced issue cognitions rather than voting behaviour.

Fourth, in four of the six countries (and most noticeably in Britain), age independently affected turn-out, with older people voting more frequently regardless of their levels of campaign involvement in other respects. This suggests that the long-standing socialisation of older citizens to the habit of voting had brought some of them to the polls, regardless of any other consideration - and especially in Britain, where the campaign was such a low-stimulus affair. Except in Germany, older people were also independently more interested in the campaign.

Fifth, campaign communication factors played a measurably independent, if sometimes modest yet often remarkably uniform, part in guiding voters' responses to the election. They apparently performed several roles in the involvement process. Level of interest in the campaign, for example, was a particularly pivotal influence. It is perhaps not surprising that it emerged from all the analyses as highly correlated with popular exposure to the campaign. But it was universally a direct influence on respondents' voting rates as well. In fact, campaign interest was the strongest direct determinant of turn-out in Britain, Holland and France. In Denmark its influence was exceeded only by another campaign factor - level of exposure to election communications. And in Germany and Ireland its impact was surpassed only by party preference variables. But in addition, exposure to campaign messages accounted for significant increments of turn-out in every country (except the Netherlands), even when campaign interest and all other tested variables were controlled. Although none of the national signs of such a possible exposure effect on turn-out was large, in surviving an exacting test they underline the power of communications to bring into the voting booths a number of people who probably would not have arrived there by any other route. Furthermore, over and above the role of interest and exposure, evaluations of the television campaign were significantly associated with turn-out in three countries:

		Beta weight
Denmark	- number of positive statements endorsed about the campaign	.10
	- number of criticisms of the campaign endorsed	-.12
Netherlands	- number of criticisms endorsed	-.12
Ireland	- number of criticisms endorsed	-.05

Although this pattern is not universal, and the beta weights are not high, there is at least a sign here that for some Europeans an unfavourable impression of the May/June campaign could itself have inhibited voting.

Campaign influences were apparently even more important in engendering an awareness of the election issues than they had been in stimulating voting. Exposure to the campaign was often a quite impressively powerful source of such a development (except in Denmark where it barely reached a statistically significant level). In five countries (Belgium, France, Ireland, Italy and the Netherlands), the amount of election material people consumed accounted for more variance in the number of issues that they could mention than did any other factor in the entire analysis, and in the Dutch sample the beta weight for this association reached .31. And in contrast to its role in turn-out, where the impact of exposure was typically subordinate to that of interest, for issue awareness amount of exposure more often emerged as the dominant campaign influence (although election interest was also a statistially significant concomitant of such awareness in every sample). The following summary figures illustrate the pattern:

	From campaign interest	From campaign exposure
Eight-country average of beta weights connecting campaign influences to issue awareness	.16	.19
Six-country average of beta weights connecting campaign influences to turn-out	.24	.10

Yet evaluations of the television campaign were additionally associated with the formation of issue cognitions in five countries, the beta weights involved proving quite high in the Netherlands and France especially.

Finally, the results intriguingly flouted one central premise of the original model. Issue awareness certainly did not emerge from the analyses as a necessary pre-condition of turn-out at the polls. Direct (and weak) paths between these outcomes appeared only in the analyses for Denmark (.09), the Netherlands (.08) and Britain (.07). This finding is somewhat surprising, since, before regression controls had been applied, the raw correlations of issue awareness with voting rates were typically fairly high:

Britain	-	.29
Netherlands	-	.21
Germany	-	.20
Denmark	-	.19
France	-	.14
Ireland	-	.14

Close inspection of the detailed results showed that these correlations had declined most sharply when a) the party variables and b) campaign interest were introduced into the regression equations. The lack of a statistical dependence of turn-out on issue cognitions seems to have been due, therefore, to two factors. First, different constraints had played on each outcome, so that turn-out but not issue awareness was heavily affected by party variables, while issue awareness but not turn-out was influenced by voters' educational levels. Second, the more interested people were in the campaign, the more they simultaneously learned something from it and became motivated to vote. The elements of this interpretation can be pictorially visualised as follows:

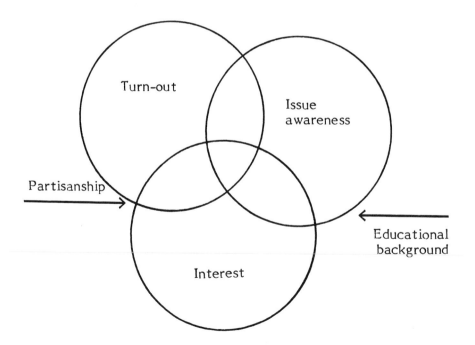

It is not that issue awareness and turn-out were unconnected. On the contrary, they were often simultaneous products of the same campaign processes. But once what those processes did for issue learning and the will to vote had been taken into account, there was little scope for the formation of issue impressions further to strengthen people's voting propensities.

A closer look at the impact of the campaign

The evidence presented so far suggests that campaign forces, in harness with those traits that had either 'politicised' or 'European-ised' individual electors, had made some contribution to turn-out and issue learning in June 1979. At least two further questions concerning the process of communication during the election still remain to be explored, however. Which <u>voters</u> were most respon-sive to the impact of the campaign? And through which <u>media</u> were their impressions of the campaign issues most often acquired and their intentions to vote most often strengthened?

Table V.2 provides a fairly consistent answer to the first of these questions. It presents the turn-out rates of sample members in six Community countries at each of several successively higher levels of exposure <u>within</u> each of four separate levels of campaign interest. In the main, the influence of exposure on turn-out appears greater at <u>lower</u> levels of interest in the campaign - as if it particularly mattered for those citizens with less-formed views who were incidentally rather than deliberately reached by election coverage. A summary expression of this tendency is provided by the gamma coefficients that are listed for the associations of exposure with turn-out for each level of campaign interest in each country. It can be seen that this coefficient was highest when calculated for those respondents who claimed to have been not at all interested in the European election campaigns that were staged in four of the countries (the exceptions being France and the Netherlands). The impact of exposure on this sub-group's voting performance was most marked in Britain, and the tendency for it to increase progressively with each step down the interest ladder was most evident in Denmark.

A similar (though less consistent) impression emerged from an identical three-way analysis of the associations of communication exposure with issue awareness at different levels of campaign interest (which is presented in full in Appendix C). It was true that the more keenly interested electors sometimes appeared more dependent on communications for learning about the issues than for resolving to vote. Nevertheless, the results for four countries (Belgium, Britain, Germany and Ireland) all tended to paint a picture of increasing issue awareness in conjunction with communication exposure at lower levels of campaign interest.

To the extent that it applies, this pattern deserves attention for several reasons. It runs counter to so-called 'knowledge gap' expectations, according to which media exposure on some topic enriches the already plentifully informed and makes them yet more different from the less engaged citizenry (Robinson, 1972). It runs counter to experience of some mass media campaigns on international topics in the past, in one of which it was concluded, for example, that '... people reached by the campaign were those least in need of it and ... the people missed by it were the audience the plan hoped to gain' (Star and Hughes, 1950). And it suggests that even in an election which was rather dismal and untidy from many points of view, with the political parties uncertain how exactly to stake out their claims to support and the broadcasters often inhibited from mounting a full-scale programming effort, the amount of comunication that was unleashed did matter in the end - perhaps imposing in this case something of a brake on what might have otherwise been an even faster decline in popular involvement in the election.

Specifically, which media played such a part? To answer that question, the regression analyses for each national sample were run again, this time substituting the individual vehicles of exposure, as a set of ten separate variables, for the composite total number of channels that had been included at the same point in the previous analyses. Table V.3 lists all those channels that survived these regressions with statistically significant paths to either turn-out or issue awareness. Amidst various other details, the results single out television as a virtually ubiquitous fount of influence in the 1979 Community election. It emerges as the only source, exposure to which affected both turn-out and issue awareness in every country without exception where the regressions assigned significant beta weights to some individual communication channel.

It appears from these results that television was a trebly important vehicle of the 1979 European election campaign. Not only did it convey election materials to more voters than were reached by any other means. Not only did it penetrate the least involved sectors of European publics more effectively than any other channel. After all other measured factors influencing the occasion had been controlled, what it injected into the campaign seemingly helped some audience members to arrive at a view of the election issues and aroused or sustained their readiness to vote as well. The long reach of this medium into the less politically motivated part of the electorate, who tended to be most open to campaign influences anyhow, probably goes some way toward explaining its distinctive role as (in these senses) the only Community-wide agency of European election communication 'effects'.

An overview of the process of election involvement

How can these detailed findings be brought together in a summary interpretation? In the Community as a whole, turn-out at the European election was largely a product of four independently operative influences. First, being a party supporter with a domestic election preference counted in all countries except Britain. Second, higher levels of interest in the campaign strongly supported turn-out in all countries. That avenue to turn-out was supported in turn by awareness of the European Parliament as a potentially effective institution, but also by being better educated, older in age and having a party preference. Third, despite the close association of campaign interest with exposure, following the campaign through the various communication channels, and especially television, independently promoted turn-out in all countries except the Netherlands, chiefly activating the otherwise less involved Europeans. And finally, in four of the six countries, age independently affected turn-out, with older people going to the polls more frequently regardless of their degree of campaign involvement in other respects. Also underlying much of this process was the consistent role of educational background, which, though nowhere a direct influence on turn-out, had strengthened certain intervening factors through which the campaign had encouraged voting participation (outlook on Europe, campaign interest and exposure). Awareness of the election issues was promoted by a somewhat different set of influences, however - for example, education rather than age or partisanship, and exposure to the campaign rather more than interest in it.

Thus, three pivotal distinctions run through the results. One of these differentiates the cognitive from the behavioural outcomes of an election campaign. From this perspective it is logical a) that issue learning should have depended more heavily on exposure to election materials, while turn-out was more the product of an affective disposition like campaign interest, as well as b) that the better-educated citizens should have been more attuned to the issues of this difficult campaign, while older people acted on their civic commitments by voting at an above-average rate.

Another distinction built into the initial model differentiated 'European' from 'non-European' routes to electoral participation. Most of the paths originally postulated for the 'European' avenue were confirmed by the regression results. But they were also supplemented by the role of several 'non-European' factors. Among these, the most important were the prior partisan commitments of many electors and the greater responsiveness to the campaign of better-educated and older voters at several stages of the involvement process.

Thirdly, it seems that we may also distinguish between those paths to involvement that originate in people's social and political situations, or in their more abiding convictions, and those that depend more contingently on the volume and appeal of message factors of the moment - particularly as they impinge on individuals who were initially less attuned to Europe on other counts. Once such a distinction is drawn, it becomes tempting to categorise certain individual countries according to the strength of the involvement impulses of both kinds that obtained in 1979. On this reckoning, Germany, perhaps, with a population that was pro-Community and a relatively active and positively valued campaign, can be classified as having been doubly involved in the 1979 election. In contrast, Britain was weak in both respects; and Belgium and the Netherlands were mixed specimens, with a high ranking for distribution of the factors promoting stable involvement of their populations, but a low one for the relatively weak communication efforts they underwent in 1979.

The distinctive campaigns

The validity of much of the foregoing interpretation is reinforced by the regression analysis results for those individual countries which diverged from the overall Community pattern in some major respect, and by our ability in such cases to trace the deviations back to distinctive features of their campaigns.

One such deviant country was Britain, where the regression pattern showed: no direct path from party preference variables to

112

turn-out; a direct path from pro-European outlook to turn-out; and a far higher beta weight for the path from campaign interest to turn-out than appeared in any other national analysis. These findings directly reflect the staging of a low-key campaign, fuelled by only minimal party efforts, which happened to take place shortly after a domestic general election, and which therefore had to focus largely on the country's relations with Europe. Such a campaign naturally suppressed the normal impact of partisan influences, heightened the role of campaign interest, and ensured that attitudes to Europe would structure much of the public response.

Other deviations appeared in the results for the Netherlands, where campaign forces seemed to operate quite differently from elsewhere. Uniquely, election exposure did not encourage voting at the polls. Yet the same factor of exposure proved outstandingly powerful in engendering an awareness of the election issues. This pattern is compatible with several features of the Dutch campaign that have emerged from other parts of our research. For one thing, the television coverage noticeably lacked a strong partisan thrust, due to the out-of-peak-time scheduling of the party broadcasts, the sparse news coverage, and the failure of the ideologically segmented broadcasting authorities to arrange many inter-party discussions and debates. It was as if the television campaign in the Netherlands was starved of those elements of partisan advocacy and rivalry that might have motivated more audience members to participate. Instead much of the burden of responsibility for coverage fell on the national umbrella organisation, NOS, which devolved this, in turn, chiefly to its foreign affairs department. This yielded a second feature of the Dutch campaign, namely, its heavy stress, in many discussion and current affairs programmes, on the provision of factual background materials on European affairs (an emphasis that had characterised the country's information campaign in the run-up period as well). This could help to explain why a considerable amount of learning occurred without appreciably boosting turn-out.

Denmark, on the other hand, diverged from the Community pattern virtually in an opposite direction from the Dutch deviation. It was only in Denmark that the campaign influences of both interest and exposure were more powerful in stimulating turn-out than in creating issue awareness. This result closely accords with the associated fact that the Danish campaign organisation was virtually a mirror image of the Dutch arrangements. For one thing, party advocacy tended to dominate the campaign on Danish television - comprising an almost nightly sequence of thirteen lengthy party broadcasts coupled with journalists putting questions to the party spokesmen concerned. For another, the Danish campaign failed to throw up a full range of election issues - concentrating largely on the single question of whether or not the country's interests were well served by remaining in the Common Market.

Some of the deviations for Germany are more difficult to explain. These included: exceptionally powerful direct paths from all the party variables to turn-out; almost equally powerful paths from the party variables to assessments of the Parliament's future impact; no direct path from age to turn-out; and a direct path from the sex factor to turn-out. The specially central role of partisanship in the German results seems to reflect the above-average investment put into the campaign by the country's major parties (Bibes, et al., 1980). Their strong emphasis on European integration may have encouraged many with party allegiances both to rate the Parliament, as its potential instrument, more highly and to go to the polls in considerable numbers. The attenuated role of age reflects below-average voting rates among the youngest and oldest citizens alike. But whereas youthful abstention was quite widespread throughout the Community, the more particular failure of older Germans to vote on polling day may have reflected their generational detachment from the pro-European mood that had captured much of the rest of the population in the post-war period. Moreover, the sex distinction suggests that a dutiful outlook on voting, which elsewhere mainly characterised older people, was in Germany a feature of male electors.

The enigma of election turn-out

Many of the findings that have been presented here help to explain the two-sided puzzle that can be posed about European voting rates in the first Community election. Why, in all the countries where voting was free from any official sanction, did voting levels fall well below those of the usual general election standard? And why, despite all the difficulties of staging a convincing campaign, did so many Europeans trouble nevertheless to vote in June 1979? The shortfall in voting participation is probably best explained by the inherently uninteresting quality of much of the preceding campaign. After all, our measure of campaign interest was the most powerful predictor of turn-out in three countries and next most powerful in another. Yet almost everywhere, only small minorities claimed that they had been 'very' or 'quite' interested in the campaign as it proceeded. Turning to the other side of the voting record coin, however, due partly to its subordination of domestic political factors and organisation, the election did not depend for its momentum solely on purely European impulses. Instead the campaign apparently unleashed a miscellany of different forces, none very powerful in its own right, perhaps, but capable in concert of prompting a tolerably sizeable turn-out. Thus, although some people voted to demonstrate their Europeanism, others went to the polls through force of voting habit and duty, others were driven by partisan loyalties, still others assumed the roles of politically more aware citizens defined by age, status or sex, and some were apparently enticed into the voting booths by communication influences per se. Many individuals in this last category were quite different from the other voters. Lacking commitment to Europe and interest in the campaign, they probably would not have made it to the polls but for the effect of communication - channelled more often than not through exposure to election programmes on television.

Cross-national system differences

So far we have mainly endeavoured to explain differences between individuals in voting propensities, not differences between countries in turn-out levels. Communications apparently affected the former, but is there any evidence to suggest that cross-national differences of campaign activity could have shaped the latter? In explaining differences of general election turn-out rates among 30 democracies, Power (1980) emphasises three forms of environmental influence (other than compulsory voting): the voting system (PR favours high voting); linkages between parties and national cleavage groups (the closer the linkage the higher the turn-out); and ease of voter registration. In the Common Market countries, such influences should have acted as constants, however, moulding behaviour at the European election and past general elections alike. Yet the following figures, extracted from Table I.1, show little match between variations of European election polling in the six countries where voting is not officially constrained and differences of citizen participation at the previous general election. (See over)

Germany is top and the UK bottom of both lists, but for the remaining countries the Euro-election pattern actually reverses the domestic election one. What system differences could account for these deviations? It looks as if influences peculiar to a European election were responsible for 'distorting' the results away from the norm in certain countries. But if so, what were they? And did campaign factors feature among them?

	European turn-out		Last general election turn-out	
	%	Rank	%	Rank
Germany	66	1	91	1
Ireland	64	2	77	5
France	61	3	81	4
Netherlands	58	4	88	3
Denmark	47	5	89	2
United Kingdom	32	6	76	6

In pursuit of some answers to these questions, we ranked the six countries according to a number of system characteristics that might have affected rates of voting participation in June 1979. In one such analysis we were looking for factors that were associated with levels of campaign communication activity (measured here by sample members' reports of communications received), and in another we were looking for factors that were associated with turn-out levels, including extent of campaign communication activity. The results may be consulted in Table V.4.

A definite, though not entirely expected, pattern emerges from these figures. Apparently, a given nation's level of communication activity did not depend on the strength of its population's attachment to Europe. Instead, this was related to its customary degree of politicisation, as measured by the extent of voting turn-out at the previous general election. European election turn-out, however, did depend both on the level of campaign communications received (especially, perhaps, through party initiatives and channels) and on the level of pro-European attitude in the public at large. The main influences that were seemingly responsible for these differences between the Community's national political systems can be visualised as follows:

Such a pattern also offers a concise explanation of the differences of national voting performance that were registered by the individual electorates in 1979. Germany's above-average turn-out

116

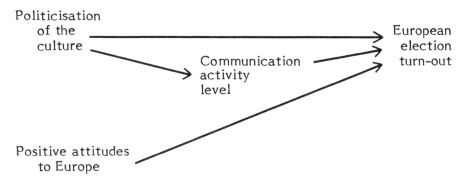

Politicisation of the culture → European election turn-out

Communication activity level

Positive attitudes to Europe

was doubly sustained: by pro-European sentiments and a relatively active campaign. Poor turn-out in Britain was attributable to the same factors in reverse: low levels of Community support and communication activity. Ireland achieved a relatively high poll chiefly in response to a keenly fought though more domestically oriented campaign. Denmark's turn-out was low, despite a relatively active campaign, because of widespread electoral reservations about the value of the Common Market. The Netherlands, on the other hand, slipped in the Euro-election voting table, despite the pro-European outlook of many Dutchmen, because of the desultory campaign that was waged there. Thus, as the Danish case shows, it was difficult for even a fairly vigorous campaign to overcome the inertia of population sectors that were initially indifferent to the European Community. But, as the Dutch case shows, a high level of mass approval could not in itself guarantee widespread electoral participation if it was not backed up by an effective campaign.

NOTES

1. Regression analysis also assumes a continuous distribution underlying the variable being measured, whereas our ultimate criterion, turn-out, is measured as a dichotomy, individuals being able only to vote or abstain. It can be argued, however, that the linear assumption of the regression model refers to an underlying propensity and hence to the conceptual definition of the dependent variable rather than to its measurement. In that case a tendency to vote rather than abstain could still be thought of as forming a continuum on the conceptual plane.

2. Some research into the quite lengthy presidential election campaigns that are held in the United States suggests that in

117

early months interest stimulates exposure, while at a later stage exposure reinforces interest (Patterson, 1980).

3. Beta weights can be derived from standardised or unstandardised regression coefficients. The results presented in this chapter are based on the former, which are regarded as more suitable for single-sample analysis because they take account of the standard errors of the variables concerned. Although they are usually thought doubtful for comparisons across samples (because a particular variable in a particular sample may be deviant for sampling reasons rather than substantive ones), inspection of the computer output showed that for each variable in the analysis the standard errors were closely similar across all national samples. In other words, the main reason for not relying on standardised coefficients in comparative analysis seemed to be obviated in the case of these data sets.

4. In the eight samples, the multiple correlation coefficients of all background variables with the measure of European outlook used was as follows:

Great Britain	-	.41
Germany	-	.29
Belgium	-	.26
Ireland	-	.23
Denmark	-	.21
France	-	.14
Netherlands	-	.14
Italy	-	.12

Table V.1   Bivariate associations of campaign interest and exposure with turn-out in six national samples

	Per cent turn-out in designated sub-groups					
	Denmark	France	Germany	Great Britain	Ireland	Nether-lands
Interest in campaign:						
Very	71	87	94	77	84	92
Quite	66	89	93	77	86	82
Little	5	76	71	46	78	71
Not at all	24	59	36	14	53	42
Exposure to campaign:						
No. of channels followed:						
6+	80	92	85	69	85	84
4-5	57	86	79	65	81	73
3	63	86	81	55	76	78
2	46	71	72	46	67	66
1	38	70	51	38	65	69
0	18	60	29	14	42	49

Table V.2　Turn-out by campaign exposure, holding interest constant

Country	Interest level	No. of channels of exposure 0	1	2	3+	Gamma coefficient
Denmark	Very	a	71	56	74	.11
	Quite	67	68	51	72	.23
	Only a little	16	39	50	60	.31
	Not at all	15	16	32	45	.42
France	Very	50	80	88	90	.22
	Quite	38	92	86	92	.24
	Only a little	69	74	66	96	.24
	Not at all	58	54	54	74	.13
Germany	Very	a	100	67	96	.18
	Quite	100	80	85	87	.09
	Only a little	20	44	65	64	.22
	Not at all	21	26	29	48	.27
Great Britain	Very	62	43	85	82	.25
	Quite	62	80	81	77	.04
	Only a little	24	42	51	54	.23
	Not at all	5	16	20	31	.51
Ireland	Very	90	75	78	87	.08
	Quite	88	87	80	86	.09
	Only a little	64	80	75	79	.06
	Not at all	40	54	53	62	.16
Netherlands	Very	71	91	64	98	.67
	Quite	85	81	74	84	.10
	Only a little	75	74	68	66	-.14
	Not at all	36	52	43	38	.11

a　No cases.

Table V.3 Statistically significant influences on election outcomes of exposure to individual channels of campaign communication

	Great Britain	Ireland	Denmark	France	Germany	Nether-lands	Belgium	Italy
				Beta weights				
TURNOUT								
Television	.12	.08	.10	.08	a	b	c	c
Conversation	.14	.08	.11					
Newspapers			.08					
Party literature				.09				
Persuading others	.10							
ISSUE AWARENESS								
Television	.10	.06	a	.11	.13	.09	.14	.07
Conversation	.13	.08			.07	.13		.13
Radio		.12		.08		.11		
Newspapers						.08		.07
Posters					.08	.09		
Party literature		.06						
Persuading others	.11							

a   No individual channel.
b   No exposure effect.
c   Not analysed (too little variance to explain).

121

Table V.4   Selected system-level correlations of national differences of communication activity and turn-out

Samples' campaign communication exposure (No. of channels)		Last election turn-out	Country rankings Per cent Eurobarometre saying Common Market a 'good thing' April 1979	Per cent Eurobarometre saying unification should be speeded up
Germany	1	1	2	1
Denmark	2	2	5	6
Ireland	3	5	4	4
France	4	4	3	3
United Kingdom	5	6	6	5
Netherlands	6	3	1	2
Rank order coefficient:		.60	-.09	.03

European election turn-out		Last election turn-out	Market membership a 'good thing'	Unity to be speeded up	Samples' campaign communication exposure No. of channels	Read party literature
Germany	1	1	2	1	1	1
Ireland	2	5	4	4	3	2
France	3	4	3	3	4	3
Netherlands	4	3	1	2	6	6
Denmark	5	2	5	6	2	5
United Kingdom	6	6	6	5	5	4
Rank order coefficient:		.43	.60	.71	.54	.77

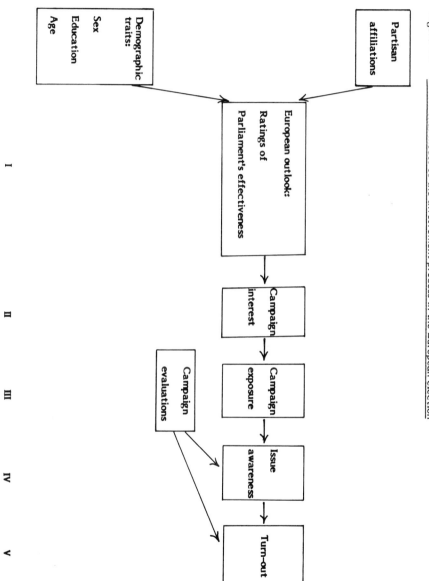

Figure V.1   Provisional model of the involvement process in the European election

I   II   III   IV   V

123

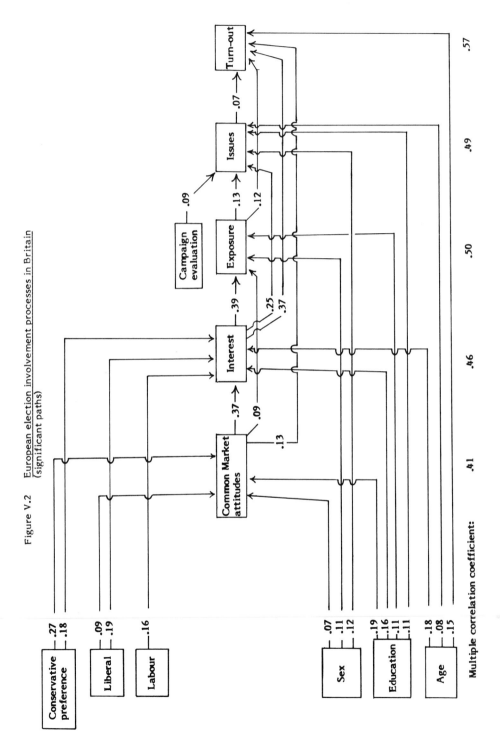

Figure V.2   European election involvement processes in Britain
(significant paths)

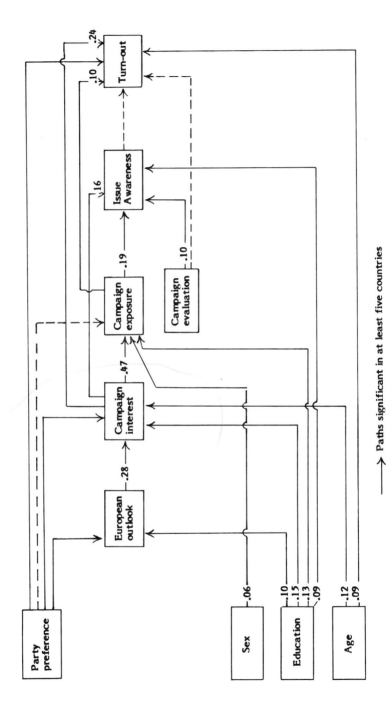

Figure V.3   Composite summary of direct and indirect influences on turn-out and issue awareness at the European elections

Turn-out

.24

.10

Issue
Awareness

.16

Campaign
exposure   .19

Campaign
evaluation   .10

Campaign
interest

.47

European
outlook

.28

Party
preference

Sex   .06

Education   .10
           .15
           .13
           .09

Age   .12
        .09

⟶ Paths significant in at least five countries

---⟶ Influential paths in some countries

125

VI A EUROPEAN ELECTION?

In this chapter we turn from the distinction between those who abstained and those who participated in the election to consider some crucial questions about the political outlook of those who did cast ballots in June 1979. How many experienced the first Community poll as a European occasion? Which voters were most inclined to take part in that spirit? Did the campaign they followed help them to perceive the voting alternatives in a European context? How far was the 'consciousness-raising' aim of the enthusiasts - to instil the idea that by going to the polls voters were engaging in a European political act - realised? In short, how ready was the European voter to turn himself into a European citizen?

Arriving at an accurate and realistic appraisal of the 1979 experience from this standpoint is important for two reasons. First, there can be no significant or durable progress toward European integration that lacks firm grounding in a supportive public mentality. Second, the chief moulders of the public consciousness - party spokesmen and mass media commentators - will be deterred from addressing electorates in European terms if they sense that the bulk of their audience will be unreceptive to messages transmitted on such a wavelength.

In a sense, though, it might hardly seem worth the trouble to sift through survey evidence to answer the questions that have been raised here. Nobody who witnessed the 1979 campaigns could plausibly claim that they were a fully supranational affair, provoking much serious discussion of the future of Europe. On the contrary, many informed observers agree first, that each national campaign had a distinctive character of its own, and second, that the level of debate was usually unimpressive. Commenting on the Belgian election, for example, Claeys et al. (1981) have concluded that:

> The double aim of exploring Europe and of clarifying party differences on its future was seldom reached, and the public usually gathered the impression that since they were all of one mind about Europe, the only criteria for determining the vote were the differences on national issues.

For France, Hollick (1979) has declared in almost identical terms that:

> The occasion of a debate about Europe's future was sadly wasted ... But, then, these elections were only incidentally about Europe.

For Ireland, it has been said that 'The campaign did not focus greatly on European issues' (Collins, 1980). In Britian, where things might have been different with the national election out of the way, the electors (according to Butler and Marquand, 1981) '... were asked to choose between more grudging Europeans and less grudging Europeans - but the lines were not clearly drawn'. From a comparative study Bibes et al. (1980) have also concluded that 'The European election campaign appeared as an extension of the domestic political debate' in Britain, France and Germany and 'as an opportunity for modifying it in ... Italy', claiming that 'national issues dominated the election and that the European issue was mainly 'instrumentalised' to serve domestic ends'. Even in Denmark, where many of the parties did line up in firmly pro-Market and anti-Market camps, the broadcasters often complained about the politicians' inability to explain 'what the election was about', their lack of comment on 'specific issues' and a tendency 'to give blurred answers to the questions put to them by journalists' (Peterson and Sauerberg, 1981). Clearly, the purist's dream of a properly European election was not realised.

The reasons for this were predominantly structural. First, the national parties closely controlled the conduct of the campaigns, relegating the transnational federations to marginal supporting roles (disseminating some literature, distributing some funds and arranging a few meetings). According to Lodge and Herman (1980), this 'nationalised what was supposed to be a supranational election'.

Second, for many political parties the salience of Europe did not automatically match the level of their support for Europe. Their main priorities and rivalries stemmed rather from the traditional economic and ideological divisions of domestic debate. Even in Belgium, where no major party disputed the value of Community membership, the key driving forces of political life had other origins - in the country's class, religious and ethnic/linguistic cleavages. And even in the Netherlands, where the Dutch Parliament had co-ordinated a substantial public information exercise in advance of the formal campaign, 'most parties compared the European election to the provincial elections at home: an interim result, not entirely reliable, but somehow vaguely indicative of the electorate's opinion of the present cabinet' (Brants, Kok and van Praag, 1979). Indeed, of the national samples of news and current affairs broadcasters interviewed by ourselves and our European colleagues, only the Germans predominantly expected the campaign to be presented on television as a 'primarily European' affair (as distinct from a 'primarily national' one or 'both' equally). Probably the Italian broadcasters would have responded in like fashion if the politicians had not decided to squeeze the European campaign into a bare week immediately after polling in the national election.(1)

Third, the relationship of the distribution of opinions on Europe to partisan cleavages was rarely conducive to staging an effective campaign with a prominent European focus. The dimensions of this problem can be appreciated by consulting Table VI.1, which shows how the supporters of major parties in eight Community countries (defined by general election voting intentions) answered the question in our post-election surveys about the benefits of Common Market membership. It can be seen that, in some countries, large parties were too internally divided over Europe to be able to pursue a particular policy line without running the risk of alienating a significant section of their own supporters. This predicament applied especially to the British parties, the French Communists and the Danish Social Democrats. In many countries, the nationally prevalent pro-European consensus, lacking a clear cross-party differentiation, could offer only a limited basis for putting on a rousing contest. Claeys et al. (1981) have defined this problem for Belgium in terms that could have been applied as well to Italy, Germany, the Netherlands, and even perhaps Ireland: '... the consensus in Belgian politics about the necessity of European integration gave little opportunity to voters to show their support or opposition to the Community'. In their study, Bibes et al. (1980)

have also drawn attention to the pressures, which are naturally generated during a national campaign to elect Members of an international assembly, for the positions of the main contenders to converge towards a consensus definition of the national interest - if only to defuse criticisms by rivals of insufficient loyalty to that interest. None of this could have been said about Denmark, however, where, alone in the EEC, a cleavage pattern of inter-party conflict and much intra-party agreement prevailed. There the voters on the far left (with opinions about the Community) were almost uniformly anti-Market in sentiment, while those backing the centre and right-wing parties were almost equally united in pro-Market support. Yet even in Denmark the polarised campaign that was fiercely fought by the more committed defenders and opponents of the European community seemed to alienate those electors who felt less strongly about these matters. Not only did supporters of the split parties (Social Democrats and Progressives) stay away from the polls in droves; among Danes with 'middle-ground' attitudes to the Common Market (regarding membership as 'neither good nor bad' or not knowing whether it benefited the country), abstention was as common as among their counterparts in Britain, where the voting was exceptionally low.2

Fourth, though for all these reasons (not to mention widespread doubts about the readiness of voters to respond to a Community-oriented campaign which was not designed to elect a Goverment) a fully European thrust could not be imparted to most campaigns, it was often realised that the outcome might have major reper-cussions on the domestic standing of the competing parties or even on the strength of rival factions and personalities within them. As Leigh (1975) has pointed out, the creation of the EEC 'has introduced new stakes into the political life of its members'. Typically, the election contestants felt obliged as a result to concoct what they hoped would be a viable mixture of domestic and European themes in their appeals to electorates. Much variety of approach and blurring of rhetoric naturally ensued; but the particular forms of 'linkage' that were forged between European-level arguments and domestically-directed claims for support differed tremendously across all the nine countries and even across the campaigns that were mounted by individual parties within each country.

If, due to overriding structural forces, then, the 1979 election could not live up to a purist's vision of a European occasion, how should we characterise it? Was it merely a set of nine 'national elections with a European face', as Hugh Thomas (cited in Butler and Marquand, 1981) has described it - or, in Hollick's (1979) terms, just a 'dress rehearsal for the (country's) next (domestic) race' - or even, as Bibes et al. (1980) have put it, 'a national election under a European pretext'?

The voters perspectives

The testimony of voters on this matter, gathered in our post-election survey interviews, is quite mixed. Overall, it tends to confirm the pre-eminent role of 'national' factors in voting decisions. Yet there were marked variations among the eight samples; in key sub-groups a more 'European' orientation was dominant; and in many cases campaign influences as such seemed to favour a European perspective.

The extent of 'European' and 'domestic' voting
The data that support these generalisations were collected from those who voted by asking them the following question:

When considering which party or candidates to vote for, which was more important for you, the parties' or candidates' stands on domestic matters or their stands on European matters?

Voters in all countries, except Germany, Italy and Denmark, were coded 'both' or 'neither', if they considered that their choices had not been made predominantly on either domestic or European grounds.

Table VI.2 provides a county-by-country overview of the bases on which respondents supposed that they had taken voting decisions. It can be seen that the number of 'domestic' voters exceeded 'European' ones everywhere. The minorities claiming to have been moved mainly by European considerations were often small, ranging from a low of 11 per cent in Ireland up to 32 per cent in Britain (looking only at the six countries where more than two answering options were presented to respondents), though rising to 35 per cent in Italy and as many as 48 per cent in Germany (where respondents were coded between just two alternatives). Those swayed at least partially by European influences often reached quite sizeable proportions, however, when the 'both' and 'European' answers were combined. In the six countries, those whose votes had some European basis ranged from 36 per cent in Belgium to around 55 per cent in Britain and the Netherlands.

Thus, a European frame of reference had at least a modest toe-hold in most electorates, though its strength was highly variable across the different countries.

Some of these cross-national divergences suggest that campaigns which differed in projecting the electoral alternatives in a more Community-oriented or a more national context may have evoked corresponding responses from their voters. One might have predicted that the more pro-European populations would have produced relatively large numbers of self-designated 'European' voters, an expectation that seems to have been borne out by the results for Germany and the Netherlands. But some of the distributions seemed to reflect the particular directions taken by national campaigns (regardless of public attitudes to the Community). Among the samples able to answer any of four ways, for example, the British one actually provided the biggest block of predominantly 'European' voters, and the next largest group of this kind was found in the Danish sample - both of which had experienced campaigns that had concentrated on the advantages and disadvantages of membership of the Common Market. Contrariwise, Irishmen were least inclined to have taken predominant account of candidates' European policy stands when voting in an election that was widely regarded as having given them an 'opportunity ... to give a mid-term verdict on the record of the Fianna Fail government to which (they) had given such a handsome victory in 1977' (Collins, 1980). The Belgian response stands out from Table VI.2 as unique in a different respect. Legally obliged to vote, those Belgians who said that they were moved by 'neither' consideration, or did not know why they had voted, amounted to almost a third of the sample (in contrast to proportions of only 7-17 per cent of elsewhere)!

Who were the European voters?
Various cross-tabular and multivariate analyses were carried out to discover who the more European-minded voters in each country were. Four main findings emerged when the voting-ground distributions were separately plotted against a number of back-ground, opinion and campaign variables.

First, many supporters of the EEC also thought of themselves as having voted a European ticket in June 1979. Some indication of this tendency is provided by Table VI.3, which shows how people's reasons for voting varied with their attitudes to the Common Market. In almost every sample, the European voters (in some

131

sense) exceeded purely domestic ones among the pro-Marketeers, while among 'middle-ground' and anti-Market voters, the pattern was usually reversed. Thus, throughout the Community, European-based voting attained or neared majority proportions among those citizens who regarded their country's membership of the Common Market as a 'good thing'. Also noticeable in the table, however, is the relative failure of Community attitudes to affect voting decisions in Ireland - another sign perhaps of the influence of those domestic impulses that had particularly fuelled much of that country's campaign.

Second, European voting decisions were associated with a higher education. In fact, of the demographic factors that were tested, only educational levels strongly and consistently differentiated people's stated reasons for voting. As Table VI.4 shows, this was a Community-wide trend, though it was most evident in Belgium, Denmark and Ireland and least marked in France and the Netherlands. Indeed, self-styled 'domestic' voters often differed little in educational attainment from those who gave 'neither' reason for voting, though the 'don't knows' to this question were least well-educated of all. So far as other background factors were concerned, men mentioned European voting grounds marginally more often than women (especially in the Netherlands and Ireland). But there was very little sign that in 1979 younger citizens felt more free or concerned to take a supranational perspective than their elders when voting - as the results of previous research by Inglehart (1977) might have predicted. Only in Britain did the younger electors tend to define themselves as European voters more often than older ones:

	18-24	25-34	35-44	55-64	65+
Per cent British respondents voting on 'European' grounds	36	40	33	30	25

It was as if in Britain's exceptionally low-key campaign, young people could stir themselves to vote only if they were specifically animated by European impulses.

Third, party support (measured by actual vote at the European election) was related to people's voting perspectives only in Britain, Denmark and France, the figures for which are presented in summary form in Table VI.5. In each of these cases, European-determined voting choices increased steadily as more right-wing parties were favoured. It can be no coincidence that these were also the three countries in which doubts and conflicting views about the compatibility of national interests with Community integration were most often ventilated by party spokesmen during the campaign. This may have had the double effect of a) influencing how traditional party supporters would contemplate the available voting option in turn and b) causing left-wing electors to shy away from giving a 'European' answer to the voting-ground question through its association in their minds with a pro-Community meaning.

Almost as interesting, however, is a factor that may have helped to level up the parties in these terms elsewhere. As Table VI.6 shows, even in most Socialist and other left-wing circles, party supporters were more likely to have turned out to vote in the European election if their attitudes to the Common Market were positive. This presumably increased the chance that, like their more right-wing counterparts, they would be moved by European considerations inside the polling booth.

Fourth, the European-oriented voters had been more positively disposed to the preceding campaign: more interested in it, more exposed to it, and more favourable in their evaluation of what they saw of it on television. Details of this trend appear in Table VI.7, where a decided gradient runs through most of the country-by-country figures, identifying the 'European' voters as having been most fully involved in the campaign, followed by those who mentioned 'both' reasons, then at a still lower level by the 'domestic' voters, while in some countries the 'neither' and 'don't know' respondents were so divorced from the campaign that they could almost be said to have gone to the polls despite it. This relationship is open to two interpretations. It could either reflect the type of person the 'European' voter was - someone who was more likely to tune into the campaign - or the impact of the campaign on him. Both explanations suggest, however, that even the unsatisfactory campaigns of 1979 conveyed a rather stronger European message than most commentators have imagined: either they influenced people to weigh the voting alternatives in a Community context, or they had more to offer those who were inclined to do so.

Finally, we sought additional insight into the sources of European perspectives on voting by examining them in a multivariate framework. Among other things, this would show whether the influences identified above were at all independently operative and not just due to their own associations with each other (for example, the relationship of campaign factors with voting grounds reflecting the already detected educational background correlates of the same distinctions). In this analysis we confined our attention to two main groups of respondents: those saying that their votes had been dictated by 'domestic' policy considerations; and those acknowledging some European influence (combining those answering 'both' and 'European' to the original question). The distinguishing features of these groups were then probed by discriminant function analysis, a procedure that is designed to identify and to rank in order the best predictors of the assignment of people to either of two pre-defined categories when multivariate controls are applied. Two such analyses were performed: one deploying only 'structural' factors to predict the voting-ground differences - namely, those of education, sex, age and the party voted for; the other adding to those variables three measures of Community opinion and two campaign involvement measures. The statistical outcomes of these procedures appear in Appendix D. In Table VI.8 here we summarise the results by showing for each national sample the order in which the influences under investigation emerged from the analyses as more or less capable of differentiating the European from the domestic voters.

The results confirm three of the findings of the cross-tabular analyses. First, they underline the tendency for supporters of the European Community to have faced their voting alternatives in European terms. The one more or less Community-wide pattern in the table picks out attitudes to Common Market membership as the most powerful predictor of the difference between European and domestic voters in four countries and a major influence in two other samples as well. Ireland is the only national exception to this rule - and strikingly so, since ratings of the Common Market were the worst predictor of all in the Irish sample. It can also be seen that in many cases the predictive power of education weakened after the opinion and campaign variables were introduced into the analysis. This suggests the presence of an overlapping influence: well-educated citizens, because they were generally more favourably disposed to the Community, were also more likely to have voted for European reasons.

Second, the cross-country split over the role of partisan factors which was previously found is also confirmed. Differences of voting direction were the best of four structural predictors of the European/domestic distinction in Britain, France and Denmark and remained important in Britain and France after five other variables were introduced into the analysis as well. Elsewhere, electors' voting grounds were less determined by their party preferences.

Third, though the ability of campaign influences to differentiate European and domestic voters is also confirmed, this association is now confined to those countries in which party factors did not play a part. In fact, a more keen interest in the campaign was the best predictor of European voting in the Netherlands and Italy and was second-best in Germany and Ireland. Thus, when Europe was a focus of partisan controversy, partisan alignment rather than general orientation to the campaign structured people's bases of voting choice. In its absence, however, there was more scope for a 'special relationship' to be forged between the campaign and the more European-minded voters. Those individuals who were more concerned to keep abreast of the campaign were also more inclined to apply a European perspective to the act of voting.

In all this, Ireland emerges from the analysis as a distinctive national case. Although, as elsewhere, Irish interest in the campaign was positively associated with European reasons for voting, exposure to the campaign was positively associated with frequency of domestic voting. As they actually received more election messages, then, Irishmen tended to respond to domestic issues in deciding how to vote. It so happens that Ireland was one of only two countries whose campaign themes were coded in our project's content analysis as having been projected on television more often in a 'domestic' than a 'European' perspective.(3) The pattern strongly suggests, then, that in Community elections the nationally domestic (or transnationally European) focus which emerges from the campaigning efforts of a country's principal political and media actors may correspondingly serve to shape the frame of electoral reference adopted by some of its more heavily exposed audience members.

Resolution of the vote

In many democracies, both North American and European, electoral behaviour has become increasingly fluid in recent years. Previously life-long partisan commitments are no longer so durable; vote-switching is more common; and more citizens are uncertain whom to support at the outset of an election and are

135

prepared to make up their minds later in the light of campaign developments (Blumler, 1979; Chaffee and Choe, 1980; Penniman, 1980). The 1979 European election arguably could have capitalised on and accelerated such trends. Parties and candidates paraded in new arenas, where the criteria of preference might have been different and the claims of old loyalties weaker. In estimating the European character of the election it would therefore be natural to enquire whether changes of voting patterns and the resolution of uncertainty were often dictated by campaign-based information and impressions about Europe.

Unfortunately, the data available for addressing this issue are less directly relevant and more scattered than we would have liked. We lack information about the pre-campaign intentions of our post-election respondents and in many cases do not reliably know how they had voted at their country's previous general election. Nevertheless, the evidence from a few countries where these short-comings are less limiting does suggest that for significant groups of electors even the 1979 European parliamentary campaigns had assisted the resolution of voting decisions.

In Britain, we were able to follow change during the campaign period in the Bristol/Manchester panel, whose members were interviewed first in early May 1979 and again after Euro-election polling day. When asked in the pre-campaign interview how they might vote at the European election, the following replies were received:

European voting intent

	%
Conservative	24
Labour	22
Liberal	4
Other	1
Don't know	34
Refused	3
Won't vote	12
	100

Thus, a large section of the panel, amounting to a third, described themselves as 'don't knows' at this early stage. Under further analysis, however, many in this group surprisingly emerged as 'considered' don't knows rather than apathetic ones. Most had voted at the recent general election, for example, and had followed it as avidly in the mass media as those who named one of the parties when asked how they would vote in June. More to the point, more of these don't knows (than the Conservative, Labour and Liberal intenders) had already heard about the impending European election, showed relatively keen interest in following the European campaign, and rated their probability of voting at the end of it as 'very likely'. And when they were asked to choose from a list of possible reasons for following the European campaign those that might apply to themselves, many more said that they were concerned 'to find out about the candidates and what they stood for' (57 per cent compared to 35 per cent among those with a declared voting intention, a statistically significant difference).

But what did these individuals do on 7 June? Their actual voting rates were just as high as those registered by electors who had stated a party preference at the first interview:

	Turn-out by May voting intent:			
	Conservative	Labour	Liberal	Don't know
Per cent voted:	49	42	50	47

And in many cases the resolution of their original indecision to vote on behalf of one party or another was systematically related to developments during the campaign period in their opinions and perceptions on European issues. Such a tendency most noticeably emerged from their answers to a series of questions about the terms of Britain's membership of the Common Market. Both in May and in June respondents were initially asked to say which of the following statements came closest to their own 'view of what Britain should do about the Common Market':

It is all right for Britain to stay in the Common Market on the present terms.

Britain must stay in the Common Market but should try hard to reform it.

Britain should propose fundamental reforms of the Common Market and should leave if they are not accepted.

Britain should get out of the Common Market no matter what.

137

Next they were asked to say which of these statements came closest to the view (in turn) of the Conservative Party, the Labour Party and the Liberal Party.

The key trends in their responses to these questions are underlined in Table VI.9 according to the particular parties these undecided electors finally voted for in June. It can be seen that many of the May 'don't knows' who eventually voted for Conservative candidates a) became convinced that Britain should try to reform the terms of Community membership without threatening to leave if not satisfied and b) became aware that this was the Conservative position on the issue as well. In contrast, those 'don't knows' who eventually voted for Labour candidates shifted in the opposite direction, slightly more often being prepared to contemplate leaving the Community and especially perceiving Labour's stand as one of threatening to get out should no 'new deal' be negotiable.

The implication of these British results seems clear. Within a campaign that concentrates on European questions, even when it does so in a half-hearted and (for many) an uninspiring way, there is a real chance that a kernel of electors can draw material from it for making up their minds and basing their choices on European considerations.

Such as it is, the post-election survey evidence from several other countries supports this impression. In Denmark, for example, there was much voting flux since the previous general election in that country in 1977. Of those Danes who cast ballots at that earlier election, only 37 per cent voted for the same party again in 1979, 12 per cent backed the People's Movement against the Common Market, 12 per cent switched to some other party list and 33 per cent abstained. And (as one might expect) the list of the People's Movement against the Common Market drew virtually all its support from those electors who believed that Danish membership of the Community was a 'bad thing'. As Table VI.10 shows, holders of all other attitudes to the EEC - even lukewarm 'middleground' ones - almost invariably shunned the anti-Market movement. But among the convinced opponents, fractions that ranged from about a fifth to three-quarters of the former voters of other parties (with one exception) gravitated to the anti-Market list in 1979. Even those individuals who changed voting support between the other parties appeared sensitive to certain features of the Danish campaign. In contrast to the stable electors (those voting for the same party in both 1977 and 1979), for example, they said significantly more often that the campaign had helped them to decide how to vote (24 per cent compared to 12 per cent) and were somewhat more inclined to take account of the parties' European policy stands when voting (36 per cent compared to 29 per cent).

In France too there was considerable voting turn-over since the parliamentary election of 1978. For example, as many as 30 per cent of the Socialist voters of that year and 17 per cent of the Communists transferred their support to some other party at the European election, while a multiplication of options fragmented the right-wing vote of two years earlier:

	1978 vote		
European vote	Republican	RPR	Other right- wing parties
	%	%	%
Veil list	58	38	49
Chirac list	12	35	9
Other	11	11	19
No vote	20	16	23
N =	98	152	39

Moreover, as Table VI.11 suggests, in these circumstances the campaign did enable many Frenchmen to align their June 1979 votes with certain of their European opinions. The Socialist Party, for example, mainly retained the support of those of its previous voters who regarded French membership of the Common Market as a 'good thing'. Communist voting, on the other hand, depended most noticeably on attitudes to European integration, the loyal Communist supporters tending to feel that the process of unification should be slowed down. The same opinion variable structured the European voting choices of former Republican voters in an opposite way, such that those who favoured a speedier unification tended to prefer the Veil list; while among those individuals who backed the RPR at the previous election, attitudes to Common Market membership seemed decisive. Overall, it appears that 'the spectacular reversal of forces in favour of the Presidential party' (Bibes, et al. 1980) owed much to its ability to attract the support of Frenchmen with relatively positive attitudes to the European Community. This is in line with the responses of voters for the two competing right-wing lists to the question about the grounds of their voting decisions. Nearly two-thirds of the Veil

139

supporters said they were at least partially influenced by the candidates' European policy stands, compared with less than a half of the Chirac supporters.

Even in Ireland (the only other country where a similar analysis could be undertaken on the basis of how respondents said they had voted at the previous election of 1977) a few signs (albeit slight) pointed in the same direction. Altogether 16 per cent of the Irish electors who voted in 1977 changed allegiance in 1979, and on average they were as positive in Community attitude and as frequently exposed to the mass media campaign as were their more stable counterparts. Moreover, they expressed a significantly more keen interest in the campaign (53 per cent having described themselves as 'very' or 'quite' interested in it compared to only 37 per cent of the stable voters). And they included a few more individuals who claimed to have decided how to vote on European grounds - though the actual figures here reflect the low overall levels that were typical of the Irish electoral response (17 per cent among the switchers and 9 per cent among the stable Irish voters.

What kind of an election?

A satisfactory answer to this question must start from a recognition that in 1979 the tensions between the centripetal and centrifugal forces buffeting the European Community were not resolved. Viewed from that standpoint, its first venture on to the hustings was essentially an ambiguous election. Each campaign was nationally unique: in that sense it was not an integrated election. Party arguments and public debate rarely identified issues central to the future of Europe: in that sense it was not much of a Community election. When casting ballots many voters evidently responded to a domestic party loyalties: in that sense it was not a fully transnational election.

Yet on the basis of the evidence examined in the foregoing pages it would be inappropriate to dismiss it as a mere assemblage of nine domestic contests held simultaneously. European aware-ness (as we say in Chapter V) was a prime initial source of much electoral involvement in the campaign. Within many partisan sub-sectors, often including even the more divided Socialist circles, citizens holding a more favourable view of the EEC also partic ipated more fully in the election, up to and including a readiness to turn out on polling day. In most countries majorities or near majorities of the Community's most staunch supporters also claimed to have cast ballots wholly or in part with European considerations in mind. Many 'European' voters in that sense also reacted to the campaign as if it had had something special to offer them. And, where they could be detected, those who switched votes in this election away from a past commitment often seemed sensitive to one or more indicators of Europeanism. Despite its evident lack of connection to an agreed agenda of Community issues, this was perhaps not a wholly ineffectual showing for the tidal pull of European influences on the first election of this kind.

Another key to the tensions and essence of the election is 'linkage' (Leigh, 1975). The national campaigns, firmly in the hands of national party organisations, varied tremedously in vigour, focus and direction, and drew much of their impetus from the spur of domestic rivalry. Yet in the end they were competing for votes to send MEPs to Strasbourg, and preliminary results from analysis of politicians' remarks in campaign programmes on televisoin suggest that in a majority of cases they were obliged to put their arguments in some form of European perspective. Viewed in that light, the 1979 exercise might be most appropriately termed an ethnocentrically European election.

NOTES

1   The Parliamentary Commission, which regulated election broadcasting in Italy, virtually obliged RAI to refrain from the production of European election programmes until the national general election was out of the way.

2.   65 per cent of the 'middle-ground' Danes failed to go to the polls compared with 64 per cent of the equivalent British sample members.

3.   According to this criterion, the other predominantly domestic campaign took place in France.

Table VI.1   Attitudes to Community membership by party preference

Percentages

	Good thing	Neither	Bad thing	Don't know
Belgium				
FDF-RW/VU/VVP - Regional Parties	65	18	7	9
PSC/CVP - Social Christian Parties	62	21	-	17
PRLW-PLP/PVV - Liberal Parties	60	26	1	13
PS/BSP - Socialist Parties	48	37	3	13
Denmark				
CD - Centre Democrats	82	9	4	4
Venstre - Liberal Party	75	13	2	10
KF - Conservative Party	65	18	8	8
RV - Radical Liberal Party	52	16	10	23
Fremskridtspartiet - Progress Party	37	25	25	12
S - Social Democrat Party	34	25	36	15
VS - Left Socialist Party	5	7	80	7
SF - Socialist People's Party	4	18	67	12
DKP - Communist Party	-	4	91	4
France				
RPR - Rassemblement p. la Republique	70	19	6	5
PR - Republican Party	66	21	4	8
PS - Socialist Party	48	32	9	10
PCF - Communish Party	26	32	29	13
Germany				
FDP - Free Democratic Party	71	15	15	-
CDU/CSU - Christian Democrats	65	30	5	-
SDP - Social Democratic Party	61	34	4	-
Britain				
Conservative Party	56	15	24	6
Liberal Party	43	18	34	5
Labour Party	21	13	60	6
Ireland				
Fianna Fail	64	13	12	11
Fine Gael	63	10	18	8
Labour Party	43	19	27	10
Italy				
PSI - Socialist Party	84	10	2	4
DC - Christian Democratic Party	82	8	1	9
PCI - Communist Party	65	21	9	5
PR - Radical Party				
Netherlands				
VVD - People's Party for Freedom and Democracy	68	15	3	15
D'66 - Democrats '66	65	21	9	5
CDA - Christian Democratic Bloc	57	14	2	26
PvdA - Labour Party	49	16	9	26

142

Table VI.2   Voting grounds at the European election

	Italy	Germany	Denmark	Ireland	France	Britain	Belgium	Nether-lands
Per cent of sample voting	95	75	50	69	76	42	86	66
Per cent of sample voters saying they voted for:								
Domestic reasons	65	52	50	45	43	37	32	30
European reasons	35	48	28	11	22	32	15	26
Both	-	-	16	32	22	23	21	28
Neither	-	-	-	7	11	4	19	7
Don't know	-	-	7	4	2	4	13	10

Table VI.3   Voting grounds by attitudes to the Common Market

Percentages

| | Voting grounds | Common Market ratings: | | | |
		Good thing	Neither	Bad thing	Don't know
Belgium	European/Both	47	27	35	12
	Domestic	34	35	22	24
	Neither/Don't know	19	38	43	64
Denmark	European/Both	41	26	21	16
	Domestic	40	59	65	44
	Neither/Don't know	19	15	14	40
France	European/Both	60	26	27	27
	Domestic	31	55	60	53
	Neither/Don't know	9	19	13	20
Germany	European	53	38	31	
	Domestic	47	62	69	
Britain	European/Both	68	43	35	42
	Domestic	27	51	50	53
	Neither/Don't know	5	6	15	5
Ireland	European/Both	46	43	40	34
	Domestic	45	48	48	36
	Neither/Don't know	9	9	12	30
Italy	European	40	26	27	16
	Domestic	60	74	73	84
Netherlands	European/Both	66	43	40	27
	Domestic	24	40	43	33
	Neither/Don't know	10	17	17	40

144

Table IV.4   Educational background by voting grounds

| | Per cent leaving school at 18 or older | | | | |
| | Voting grounds | | | | Don't |
	European	Both	Domestic	Neither	know
Belgium	52	46	30	36	17
Denmark	43	22	27	a	24
France	34	46	29	22	16
Germany	28	a	16	a	a
Great Britain	23	18	15	12	7
Ireland	36	28	22	19	12
Italy	36	a	24	a	a
Netherlands	41	43	34	35	22

a   Options not offered to respondents.

145

Table VI.5   Voting grounds by direction of European vote in three countries

Britain					Labour		Liberal	Conservative
Per cent European or 'both'					41		59	64

Denmark	People's Movement against the Common Market	Left Socialist	Socialist Peoples	Social Democrats	Liberals	Conser vative	Centre Democrats
Per cent European	14	27	33	22	33	43	45

France	Communist	Socialist	Chirac list	Veil list
Per cent European or 'both'	25	47	45	57

Table VI.6 Turn-out among left-wing party supporters[a] by attitudes to the Common Market

Percentages

Membership of EC:[a]	Good thing	Neither	Bad thing	Don't know
Dutch				
PVdA	70	79	46	62
French				
Communists	87	91	83	68
Socialists	82	78	52	65
British				
Labour Party	62	35	30	37
Irish				
Labour Party	76	81	66	63
German				
SPD	82	63	67	
Danish				
CP	b	0	80	b
Left Socialists	50	33	64	33
Socialist People	100	67	85	83
Social Democrats	60	36	49	42

a   Defined by general election voting intention
b   No cases

Belgium and Italy are omitted from the table because of the very high voting rates in those countries overall.

Table VI.7   Voting grounds by campaign involvement

	Per cent 'Very' or 'Quite' interested in the campaigns				
			Voting grounds		
	European reasons	Both	Domestic reasons	Neither	Don't know
Belgium	57	44	24	12	10
Denmark	61	36	54	a	54
France	48	51	48	28	21
Germany	65	a	50	a	a
Great Britain	56	70	48	62	29
Ireland	61	43	37	25	12
Italy	43	a	23	a	a
Netherlands	59	62	37	22	16

	Average number of channels through which the campaigns were followed				
	European reasons	Both	Domestic reasons	Neither	Don't know
Belgium	3.5	3.0	2.8	3.1	1.0
Denmark	2.8	2.4	2.6		2.4
France	2.7	3.2	2.9	2.0	1.6
Germany	2.2		2.1		
Great Britain	3.5	3.0	2.8	3.1	1.0
Ireland	3.5	2.9	3.3	2.1	1.4
Italy	5.2		3.9		
Netherlands	2.7	2.9	2.1	1.3	1.1

		Average number of positive (+) and negative (-) statements endorsed about the TV campaigns					
		Belgium	Denmark	France	Germany	Great Britain	Ireland	Netherlands
European	+	1.1	1.5	0.9	1.8	1.1	1.5	0.9
	-	0.7	0.9	0.9	0.8	0.8	0.6	0.4
Both	+	1.1	1.1	1.1		1.3	1.1	1.0
	-	0.6	0.7	0.8		0.5	0.6	0.4
Domestic	+	0.8	1.2	0.9	1.5	0.8	1.1	0.5
	-	0.8	0.9	0.9	0.9	0.9	0.9	0.6
Neither	+	0.3		0.5		0.2	0.5	0.3
	-	1.1		1.4		1.2	0.9	0.6
Don't know	+	0.3	1.2	0.2		0.3	0.8	0.3
	-	0.5	0.8	0.9		0.5	0.8	0.6

a   Response options not included in these cases.

Table VI.8   Discriminant function analysis: Order of variables' ability to predict European voting(a)

	Britain	Ireland	Germany	Nether-lands	France	Italy	Denmark
Four structural variables							
Party vote	1	3	2	4	1	3	1
Sex	3	1	4*	1	2	2	4
Age	2*	4	3	2	4	4*	3
Education	4	2	1	3	3	1	2
Structural, opinion and campaign variables							
Party vote	2	4	5*	8	2	8	7
Sex	9	2	8*	2	7	9	9
Age	3*	7	9	4	6	7*	8
Education	8*	5	3	5	5	5	2
Attitudes to member-ship	1	9	1	3	1	4	1
Attitudes to uni-fication	5	6	4	7	4	6*	4
Attitudes to Parlia-ment	4	· 8	7	6	3	3	5*
Campaign interest	7	2	2	1	9	1	6*
Campaign exposure	6	1*	6	9	8	2	3

a   In most cases the coefficients showed a relationship to 'European/both' reasons for voting of positive Community opinion, higher campaign involvement, better education, male sex and older age. Asterisked numerals in the table indicate exceptions - i.e. instances when those variables went with domestic voting grounds. The party vote variable was created by grading the parties that the respondents had voted for in an order corresponding to their usual supporters' (defined by general election voting intent) attitudes to the Common Market - higher for more positive attitudes. Belgium was omitted from this table because inadequate information was obtained at the post-election interview about the parties of the candidates for whom some of the respondents had voted.

Table VI.9 Resolution of the vote on original 'don't knows' in Britain by opinions and perceptions on the terms of Common Market membership

Percentages

	Don't know to Conservative vote				Don't know to Labour vote				Don't know to Liberal vote		
	Own stand May	Own stand June	Con. stand May	Con. stand June	Own stand May	Own stand June	Lab. stand May	Lab. stand June	Own stand May	Own stand June	Lib stand May	Lib. stand June
Stay in	3	-	7	10	-	-	12	-	17	-	-	8
Reform	66	93	45	76	53	41	47	29	50	100	33	92
Leave if can't reform	24	3	14	7	24	35	12	53	25	-	25	-
Get out	-	3	7	-	18	24	6	-	-	-	-	-
Don't know	7	-	28	7	6	-	24	18	8	-	42	-

Table VI.10   Sources of anti-Market coalition voting in Denmark

Attitude to Membership of the Common Market	Per cent voting for the People's Movement against the Common Market							
	1977 vote							
	Communist	Soc. People	Social Dems.	Prog-ressive	Liberal	Conser-vative	Other	No vote
Good thing	0	0	1	0	0	0	0	0
Neither	0	0	8	6	8	5	0	3
Bad thing	74	50	32	27	0	33	26	22
Don't know	0	0	6	0	0	0	9	0
N =	25	40	341	72	106	96	124	56

Table VI.11   Inter-election voting change by European opinion in France

Previous election Socialists believing the Common Market:

European election vote	Good thing	Neither good nor bad	Bad thing	Don't know
Socialist	57	44	11	39
Other party	27	38	33	17
No vote	16	18	56	44
N =	103	61	18	18

Previous election Communists wanting European unity to be:

European election vote	Speeded up	Stay the same	Slowed down	Don't know
Communist	54	63	77	59
Other party	15	29	6	19
No vote	31	8	17	22
N =	26	58	48	27

Previous Republicans wanting European unity to be:

European election vote	Speeded up	Stay the same	Slowed down	Don't know
Veil	70	55	-	56
Chirac	15	10	33	12
Other	3	15	33	31
No vote	12	20	33	-
N =	33	40	3	16

Previous election RPR voters believing the Common Market:

European election vote	Good thing	Neither good nor bad	Bad thing	Don't know
Veil	46	15	20	43
Chirac	33	37	40	43
Other	9	19	20	-
No vote	13	30	20	14
N =	103	27	10	7

Voting reasons by Euro-vote for Veil or Chirac lists

	Veil	Chirac
European reasons	31	23
Both	32	24
Domestic reasons	26	42
Neither	7	10
Don't know	4	2
N =	109	62

VII PAST INFLUENCES AND FUTURE PROSPECTS

The first direct election to the European Parliament has emerged from this analysis of voters' reactions in the guise more of a patchwork quilt than of a seamless web. Firmly moulded by national traditions, actors and interests, yet often steering a European course of sorts, its reception in diverse demographic, partisan and opinion circles was quite uneven. And although it kindled little interest, it succeeded in the end in attracting a considerable amount of voting participation. It was thus neither a trifle nor a cataclysm; neither highly dynamic and invigorating nor entirely inert and moribund. Lacking high drama and inspiring enthusiasm in few quarters, it nevertheless set forces in motion which cannot be dismissed as utterly insignificant. Those who looked forward to the campaigns in faith, and those who approached them with scepticism, then, were both vindicated - though each only partially. In this concluding chapter, we identify four more or less distinct factors, which were particularly influential in shaping what became the mosaic of the 1979 election campaigns, and in doing so we attempt to draw together the main findings detailed in the preceding chapters.

First, as we saw in the previous chapter, attitudes to the European Community did 'pull' their 'weight' in this election. Without exaggerating their depth or force, they played a pivotal part almost everywhere, predisposing people to interest themselves in the campaign, to follow it more extensively, to learn something about the issues it raised, to vote at the end of it and to face their ballot-box choices in a more or less European frame of mind. To that extent, the European election demonstrated its potential to activate Community-oriented opinions and so justified some of the hopes invested in it in advance. The sheer fact that this was a European election, or an election of representatives to sit in a European assembly, helped to mobilise participation according to the views on Community affairs that people already held or had formed during the campaign.

But if the thread of pro-Community opinion was thus a unifying feature of the 1979 election, it was at several points manifestly thin, perhaps even dangerously close to breaking point. One sign of weakness was its uneven reach and especially its lack of appeal to many of the younger, less educated and left-wing electors of Europe. In particular, the campaign's inability to arouse those holding negative or 'middle-ground' views measured the extent to which the Common Market had not yet become a fully-fledged Community or a fully legitimated polity. Equally serious was the virtual absence of competing sets of more or less coherent alternative goals and policies for electors to grasp, support and rely on as voting guides. Neither individual MEPs nor the Parliament as a whole could realistically claim to have emerged from the 1979 election with a mandate to pursue any specific course of Community advance. Underlying all such limitations, however, was 'the basic institutional and political weakness of the European Parliament' itself (Pridham and Pridham, 1981). The goodwill of sometimes large majorities towards the Community principle was in sharp contrast to the shadowy standing of a Parliament whose political role was limited and unclear and, in the immediate future at least, was unlikely to be dramatically strengthened. Its marginality as a decision-taking body not only weakened the incentives for the competing parties to pull out all their campaign stops and caused some broadcasters to question the election's claims to much programming attention (Blumler, 1979), it was also inhibiting to the electorate. Insofar as people took the Parliament seriously, they were also prepared to involve themselves more fully in the campaign. But in most countries about a half of the electorate considered that the elected Parliament would have 'not much effect' or 'no effect at all' on their lives - or had no idea what to expect.

Second, the predominantly national control of the election arrangements yielded in turn a set of quite varied campaigns, which differed markedly in vigour, focus, content and style - and therefore in electoral reaction - from one country to another. Although it is true that the campaigns often provided vehicles for pro-European opinion tendencies to express themselves, it was as if such impulses were carried in coaches of nine different hues. Our evidence suggests that, insofar as there was a single most important initiating, and diversifying, force at work in the European election (nurtured no doubt by feed-back loops from other influences), it was the extent and form of leadership offered by the campaigning politicians and their party headquarters. They set tones from which much else followed. As the results of the regression analyses presented in Chapter V show, partisanship itself had an important bearing on electoral participation in all countries except Britain. In addition, differences of party electioneering seemed largely responsible for such distinctive outcomes as:

the striking failure to mobilise the large body of anti-Community opinion in Britain;

the (contrasting) polarisation of pro- and anti-Market forces in the Danish electorate;

the failure of the Dutch and Belgian campaigns to excite responses commensurate with their publics' prior levels of Community support;

the largely domestic slant of the campaign in Ireland;

the division of the centre/right-wing vote between the Veil and Chirac lists in France;

the exceptionally European orientation of German voters' responses to the campaign; and

the subordination of the Italian campaign to the preceding domestic election.

This is not to imply that when planning their campaigns the political parties took decisions de novo in environmentally autonomous circumstances. Campaign strategies evidently reflected the interplay of day-to-day party management concerns and resource allocations and compelling domestic priorities, as well as the problems posed by a new level of electoral contest. Differences of political systems and cultures also influenced party behaviours. There can be little doubt, for example, that the state funding made available to the German political parties provided material incentives to active campaigning which were less forceful in countries where parties had to rely more on their own treasuries. But such factors still do not explain those more qualitative differences of campaign direction, which were a legacy of the role that European questions had played in each country's national politics in the years preceding 1979, influenced by the parties' assessments of broader public attitudes to the EEC. For example, the Danish confrontation over the costs and benefits of Community membership reflected in part the long-standing tendency for Left-Right divisions to structure foreign policy debate in that country - including, of course, the conduct of the 1971 Referendum argument - and in part the prevalence of negative mass attitudes to integration, on which the Left could seek to capitalise (Schou, 1981). On the other hand (and in complete contrast), the German campaign reflected the major parties' shared commitments to the promotion of European integration, including the holding of direct elections and even pressure to increase the powers of the European Parliament. Meeting little overt resistance from the German population, it was natural for the CDU and the SPD to compete largely over which was the more European party and which could project a more attractive vision of the Community's political future (Lodge, 1981). Although a cross-party consensus towards the Community also prevailed in Ireland, the more domestic emphasis of its campaign stemmed not only from the government's mid-term unpopularity, ripe for exploitation, but also from a 'political culture which places a high premium on local politics and local personalities' and in which 'different approaches to foreign policy issues are not widely appreciated among the electorate at large' (Moxon-Browne, 1981).

Similarly, the truncated Italian campaign, virtually submerged by its domestic predecessor, emanated from a situation in which many leading politicans, though highly supportive of the Common Market, had traditionally 'given limited attention to European questions', partly because they could exercise so little influence in Community institutions (Cotta, 1918). In France, the sometimes confusing campaign (Hollick, 1979) was dominated by the need felt by a moderately pro-European centrist President to repel a challenge rooted in two decades of sceptical Gaullist nationalism. Finally, Britain's lack-lustre campaign owed much to the Labour Party's prolonged record of ambivalence and reserve towards the Common Market. Labour's indifference invited, in turn, a low-key response from the Conservatives, who, confident of victory from the outset, resolved not to arouse their lethargic opponents and run the risk of antagonising doubters in their own ranks.

In many cases, then, the 1979 campaigns waged by the politicians reflected and reinforced already established patterns of partisan response to Community affairs. But as a 'second-order' election from which no government would emerge (Reif and Schmitt, 1980), party energies, leaders and resources were not always deployed with conviction and commitment. And where the resulting effort fell far short of general election standards - as in Holland and Britain and possibly Belgium - mass involvement and even the public standing of the EEC was liable to suffer.

Many politicians and journalists would probably claim that the staging of a low-key campaign was either an inevitable or a prudent response to a third formative influence on the election: the decidedly limited motivation of the average citizen to follow European affairs in any sustained way. It would be difficult to challenge this interpretation on the basis of the post-election survey data. The low public salience of the event was ubiquitously manifested in:

the large majorities who declared themselves only a 'little interested' in the campaigns at best;

the confusion over the final outcome of the election at the Community level;

the widespread lack of awareness of any election issue;

the rather grudging gains that were registered on other points of information during the campaign;

and the strikingly low levels of endorsement of both positive and negative statements about the television coverage, as if few people had absorbed enough material even to form a judgement about its quality.

It could be counter-argued, of course, that a different kind of campaign would have evoked a different form of response. By tailoring activity to a perception of the audience as essentially unmotivated, the vicious circle of desultory campaigning matched by indifferent responses simply could not have been overcome. And the subdued domestication of election presentation may have prevented its potentially innovative international content from shining through clearly and attractively (Davis, 1980). Yet few of our respondents - except in Britain and Italy - thought that their

157

appetites for election programing had been underestimated by the campaign planners.

Fourth, however - partly because so many Community citizens lacked fully-formed and detailed prior beliefs about European questions - communication itself played a central, though varied, part in the first direct election to the European Parliament. In fact, the evidence sifted in previous chapters identifies several different lines along which communication influences may have affected popular consciousness and behaviour in June 1979.

For one thing, it apparently mattered greatly whether Europeans found the election campaign interest-worthy. It is not possible to say definitively what that criterion implies, but it may draw our attention to certain qualities which the 1979 campaigns often lacked: a sense of personal relevance; clarity of choice; an airing of key issues at stake in the outcome; and avoidance of an unduly messy confusion of European and domestic components of partisan competition.

For another, the amount of communication activity generated by the campaigns also mattered. This proposition is applicable to the levels of both individual voters and national electorates alike. Not only do the regression analyses reported in Chapter V show independent influences of the extent of campaign exposure on individual electors' awareness of campaign issues and likelihood of voting; but, with only one deviant case (that of Denmark), those systems in which people were reached by greater amounts of election materials were also those which recorded levels of turn-out most comparable to their general election standards. The cautionary examples of the Netherlands and Belgium, whose sampled respondents recalled relatively low levels of exposure to election messages, seem especially to highlight the risks involved when the chief providers of political communication do not take the campaign all that seriously. For, despite high initial levels of public acceptance of the community, turn-out in the Netherlands and issue awareness in Belgium were comparatively poor, outcomes which were accompanied by appreciable reductions in the number of committed supporters of Common Market membership as well.

In addition, the contrast between the Dutch and Danish regression analysis results points to another line of communication influence. The results imply that popular responses may depend on the form of political message that is most heavily relayed.

Denmark's greater emphasis on partisan-persuasive communications appears to have had more impact on behavioural participation in the election; while the Netherlands' more neutral-informative style of campaign was seemingly more productive of learning gain.

Finally, there were several signs that campaigns which differed in projecting the electoral alternatives in a more European or more domestic context had evoked corresponding responses from some of their voters. It will be recalled that, at the individual level, campaign communication variables were often associated with balloting on ostensibly European grounds, though in the significant case of Ireland, exposure to its decidedly more domestic campaign was associated in turn with a higher frequency of domestically-determined voting decisions. Similarly, at the aggregate level of national electorates, the overall amount of 'European' voting claimed by respondents seemed more reflective of the kinds of campaigns which they had witnessed than of the level of pro-Community opinion usually prevalent in the countries concerned.

Despite these communication influences, some of them favouring voting participation, modes learning, and the intrusion of a vaguely 'European' spirit into voting decisions, the 1979 election fell well short of initial hopes in two major respects: it was quite weak in involvement-appeal; and it made no noticeable contribution to the cultivation of a Community-wide political outlook across national boundaries. What are the chances that these shortcomings could be overcome in 1984? And whose responsibility might it be to put on a more inspiring and more meaningful campaign the next time round?

The only realistic answer to the first question, it seems to us, must be 'slim'. To stand a chance of transcending the 1979 experience, the campaign dialogue must focus, first and foremost, on alternatives which the mass of voters can clearly see could matter to their welfare, and which those seeking election could effectively pursue during the next parliamentary term. Such a diagnosis suggests a) that insofar as the 1979 election failed, it was because political conditions were unpropitious, and b) that before further elections of this kind could take off more impressively, structural reform might be necessary. In theory, various structural changes could help to do the trick: a shift to federalism in the relationship between Community and national-governmental institutions; a transfer of campaigning powers to the transnational party

159

federations; or the acquisition by the European Parliament of new roles and powers for itself in Community government (Blumler and Fox, 1980). But such approaches are out of line with the process of Community evolution to date, whereby minimal incrementalism, not dramatic stuctural change, has governed the pace of political advance (Pridham and Pridham, 1981). Even the 'long and difficult road to (the holding of) European elections' (Patijn, 1975) took two decades to travel. According to informed observers, it is 'highly unlikely', except on minor points, 'that the 1984 direct elections will be conducted according to a common electoral law'. Consequently, it can take on a more European character only 'through the way (it is) conducted and fought ... by national parties and transnational party federations' (Herman and Lodge, 1981). Yet there is little reason to expect the former to cede much extra jurisdiction to the latter. And although in future years Community policies may gather momentum in wider fields and impinge more directly on the national politics of member states, so long as the resulting issues continue to be fought out and decided chiefly in inter-governmental fora, such as the Council of Ministers, the process of direct election to a peripheral Parliament may still fail to come fully to life.

There is one new factor in the equation that could make some difference in 1984. Previously elected MEPs will be standing for re-election and fighting opponents attempting to unseat them. The 1984 campaigns may not have to depend so heavily, then, as in 1979 on a refurbishing of the rival parties' traditional Community attitudes, and could be enlivened by the availability of parliamentary records to defend and attack. Whether this will make a real difference, however, must depend on the actual records that incumbents build up before 1984, how these relate to electors' concerns and interests, and whether the Parliament has in the meantime strengthened its political muscle in Community decision-taking.

In all this it is not easy to assign responsibilities for mounting a satisfying campaign, partly because election communication is itself a subtly composite product, fusing the contributions of politicians and journalists who to a considerable extent are continually adapting and reacting to each other (Blumler and Gurevitch, forthcoming). The resulting chicken-and-egg dilemma is well illustrated by Butler and Marquand's (1981) reflections on the 1979 campaign in Britain:

The politicians were not trying very hard. One reason for this is that the media were not reporting them or encouraging them to think the public was interested (although the media could ripost that it was the politicians' fault for not saying or doing newsworthy things).

Of course the mass media do carry important responsibilities at election time. They should not prematurely surround an impending election with such a pervasive miasma of jaded scepticism that not even an army of dedicated campaigners can sweep it away. In the case of a European election, involving unfamiliar and remote institutions, the informing mission of the media must be particularly vital - as is their less often mentioned 'correlation function'. In a nine-nation election, inevitably attracting many scattered contributions, aimed at confusingly divergent targets, they alone can try to focus the argument and so help the citizen-audience member to put it together for himself. And in 1984 especially, they should aim to ensure that parliamentary candidates enjoy sufficient access to air their own views and experiences - a need that was clearly neglected in some countries in 1979.(1)

In the final analysis, however, professional communicators must depend heavily on the kind of lead that the electioneering politicians give. Partly this is because their pronouncements, activities and arguments provide the basic raw materials of much campaign programming and press reporting. Partly it is because, in many of Europe's public service broadcasting systems, the parties have some voice in actually deciding how television (undoubtedly the most important vehicle of European election communication) will present a campaign. Partly it arises from an ethic that has developed in recent years of a subordination at election time of the broadcasters' independent agenda-setting functions to party initiatives, on the ground that electors ultimately choose between politicans and not broadcasters when deciding how to vote (Blumler, Gurevitch and Ives, 1978). But most important of all, it is because, if party efforts are half-hearted, it is bound to take the heart out of an election so far as the public is concerned as well. It is all very well for broadcasters and other journalists to try to develop streams of educative material, concentrating on the provision of background information for conscientious votes. Such an effort, however skilfully mounted, can only give people a certain amount of knowledge and not a will to act. Though it may inform them, it cannot motivate them. It is the politicians alone who can not only offer members of the public an ordering of issue priorities and policy alternatives to choose between but also present such options in a way that makes the choice seem to matter. Such a function is vital to any electoral process - and in 1984 only the political parties and their candidates will be able to discharge it.

NOTES

1. According to the wider project's analysis of campaign content on television, candidates standing for the European Parliament received only 10 per cent of the total programming time in Germany, 1 per cent in Britain, 12 per cent in Luxembourg, 14 per cent in Italy, and 17 per cent in the Netherlands, rising to 28 per cent in Denmark, 38 per cent in France and 54 per cent in Belgium.

APPENDIX A

The Questionnaire

Qn.1 Thinking back to just before the elections for the European Parliament were held, how interested were you in the campaign for those elections - would you say you were very interested, quite interested, only a little interested, or not interested in it at all?

Qn.2 Leaving aside which party did best here in _____, do you know which group of parties won the largest number of seats in the European Parliament as a whole?

    Communists and their allies
    Socialists
    Liberal and Democratic Group
    Christian Democrats
    European Conservatives
    European Progressive Democrats
    Others (please specify)
    Don't know

Qn.3 Which of the following did you do during the two or three weeks before the European elections? Which others? (Show Card and mark all mentioned).

    CARD A
    Talked to friends, family or workmates about the European elections
    Spoke to a political party worker about the European elections
    Attended a public meeting or rally about the elections
    Read European elections material sent to my home by a party or candidate
    Read a poster about the European elections
    Read an advertisement in a newspaper or magazine about the elections
    Read a newspaper report about the European elections
    Watched a programme about the European elections on television
    Heard a programme about the European elections on the radio

Tried to persuade somebody to vote for a party or candidate in the European elections.

On.4 What do you think were the most important issues that emerged during the European elections?   Anything else? (Write in reply and code)

a   Agricultural policy, fishing, food-mountains
b   Unemployment, jobs, work opportunities
c   Prices, inflation, cost of living
d   Energy, nuclear power, conservation and use of natural resources
e   Regional and urban development, regional fund, regional needs
f   Protection of national independence, sovereignty and culture; avoidance of supra-nationalism
g   Social policies, social services and human rights; status of women and minorities
h   Stronger democratic control of EC, powers of the European Parliament, control of bureaucracy
i   Greater European co-operation, unity, avoidance of war; European ideals and consciousness
j   International relations, Europe as a world power security, relations with other powers and third world
k   Political preferences for Europe; the ideological future of Europe - capitalist/conservative/social-ist/anti-socialist/christian democratic, etc.
l   Other reply (please specify)

Qn.5 How often did you watch any television programme or television news report about the European election campaign during the two or three weeks before the election - every day, almost every day, from time to time, or not at all?

Qn.6 Thinking especially about how the campaign was covered on television, which of these statements would you say you agree with?
(Show Card and mark all mentioned)

CARD B
a   It helped me to make up my mind how to vote
b   It didn't tell me about the advantages and disadvantages of _____ being in Europe

164

c It showed me where my party stands on European questions
d It didn't show me why I should care about the European Parliament
e It brought out well the main differences between the parties on European matters
f It told me how the European Community is run
g It all seemed rather boring
h It helped me to think more about the future of Europe
i It left me feeling rather confused
j It told me about the relationship between _____ parties and those in other European countries.

Qn.7 Overall, how do you feel about the amount of time devoted to the European election campaign on television - would you say that far too much time was spent on it, a bit too much, about the right amount, or not enough time?

Qn.8 Thinking about the future, how much effect do you think what the European Parliament does will have on people like yourself - a great effect, some effect, not much effect, or no effect at all?

Qn.9 Generally speaking, do you think that _____'s membership of the Common Market is a good thing, a bad thing, or neither good nor bad?

Qn.10 Some people think of the Common Market as being a first step towards a closer union between the member states. Do you think that the unification of Europe should be speeded up, slowed down, or continued as at present?

Qn.11 In most elections a lot of people do not vote for one reason or another. How about you, did you vote in the European elections? If 'YES': Which party did you vote for?

Qn.12 When considering which party or candidate to vote for, which was more important to you, the parties' or candidates' stands on dometic matters or their stands on European matters?

Qn.13 ASKED OF NON-VOTERS ONLY: Which would you say was the main reason that you did not vote? (Show Card)

165

CARD C
a   Was not eligible to vote
b   Personal reasons: sickness, holiday, business commit-
    ments
c   Lack of interest in politics/elections
d   Lack of interest in European elections, European
    Parliament, European affairs
e   Hostility to European institutions or ties with Europe
f   Not informed enough to vote in the European election
g   There was no party or candidate that I could support
h   Thought the result was a foregone conclusion
i   Didn't realise there was an election
j   Other reply (please specify)

Qn.14 Do you remember whether you voted in the last general
      election held in _____?
      IF 'YES': which party did you vote for in that election?

166

APPENDIX B

<u>European election involvement processes in</u>:

Belgium
Denmark
France
Germany
Ireland
Italy
The Netherlands

<u>Statistically significant paths from regression analysis results</u>

BELGIUM

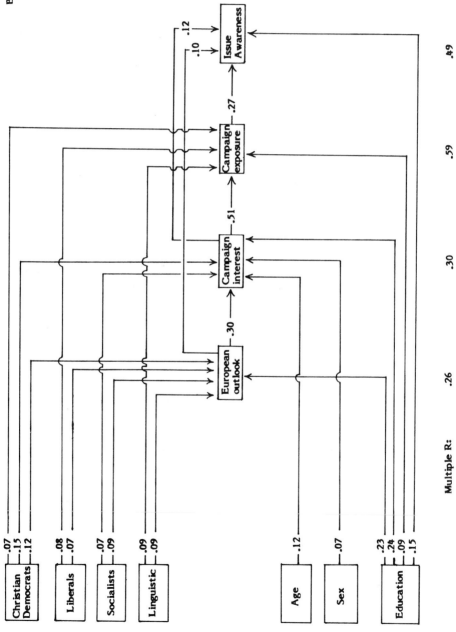

Multiple R:	.26	.30	.59	.49	

168

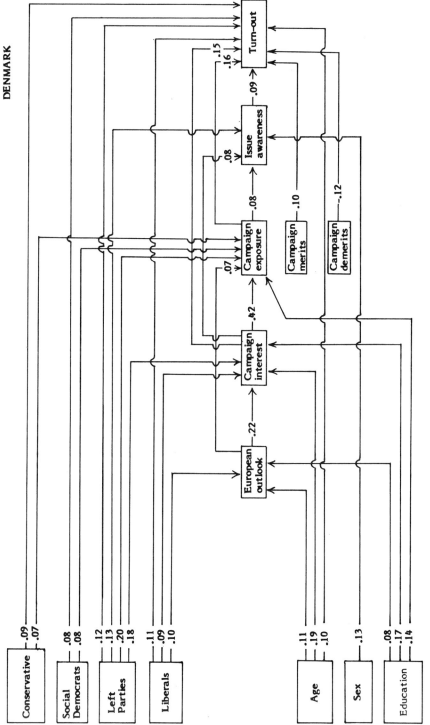

DENMARK

Multiple R: .47   .27   .56   .36   .21

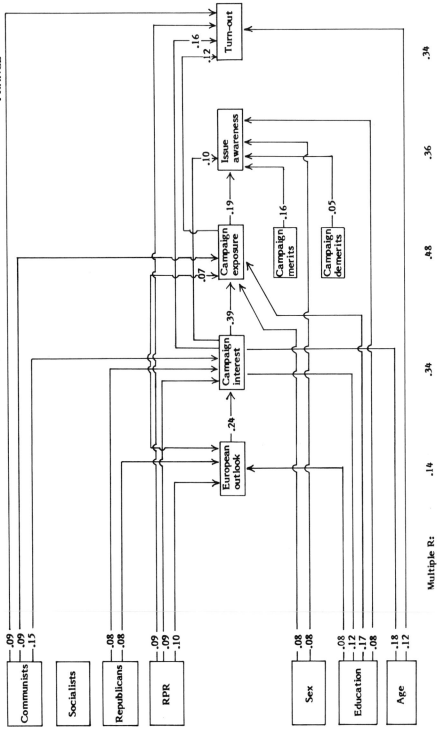

FRANCE

	.14	.34	.48	.36	.34	

Multiple R:

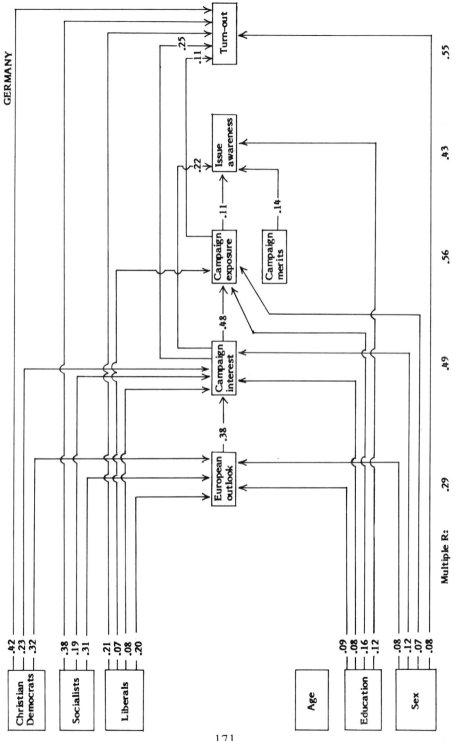

GERMANY

	Multiple R:					
	.29	.49	.56	.43	.55	

Christian Democrats: .42, .23, .32

Socialists: .38, .19, .31

Liberals: .21, .07, .08, .20

Age:

Education: .09, .08, .16, .12

Sex: .08, .12, .07, .08

European outlook — .38 → Campaign interest — .48 → Campaign exposure — .11 → Issue awareness

Campaign merits — .14

Campaign exposure — .11 → Turn-out

.22

.25

.11

Turn-out

171

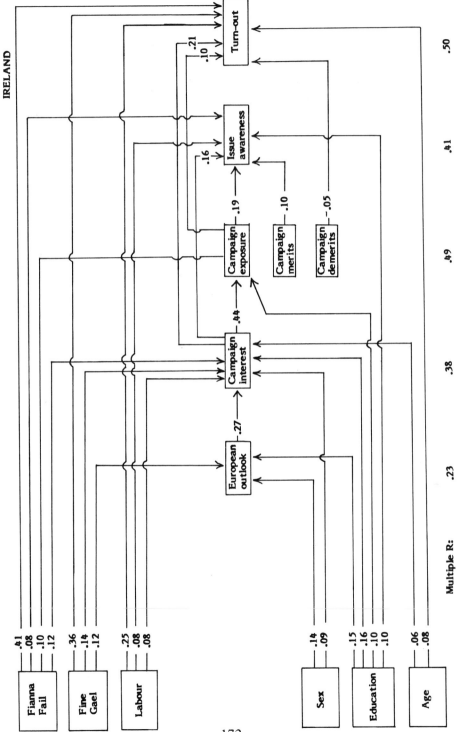

IRELAND

172

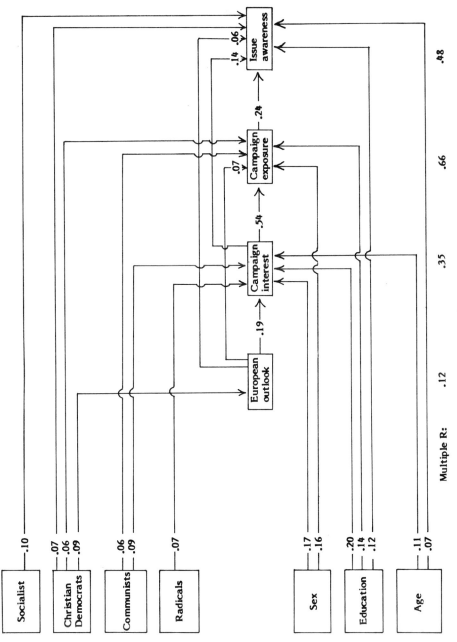

ITALY

173

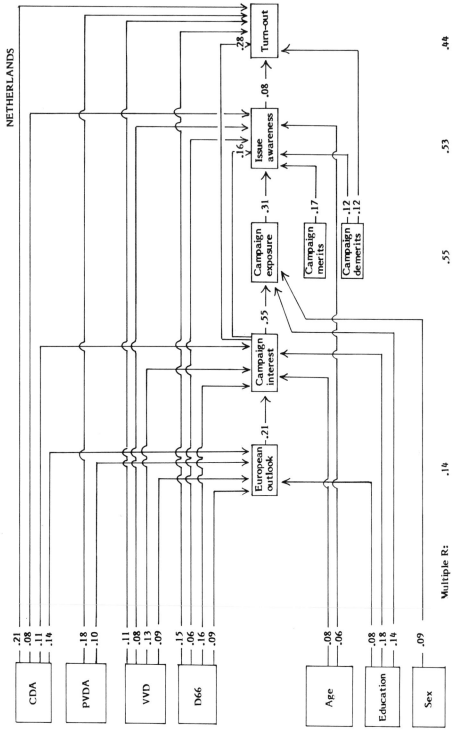

NETHERLANDS

CDA	.21 .08 .11 .14	
PVDA	.18 .10	
VVD	.11 .08 .13 .09	
D66	.15 .06 .16 .09	
Age	.08 .06	
Education	.08 .18 .14	
Sex	.09	

European outlook → .21 → Campaign interest → .55 → Campaign exposure → .31 → Issue awareness → .08 → Turn-out

.16 → Issue awareness

.28 → Turn-out

Campaign merits → .17

Campaign demerits → .12 .12

Multiple R: .14   .55   .53   .44

174

APPENDIX C

Average number of European election issues mentioned by campaign interest and exposure

Country	Campaign interest	Exposure: number of channels			
		0	1	2	3+
Belgium	very	0.5	1.2	1.0	1.4
	quite	0.4	0.8	1.1.	1.1
	only a little	0.1	0.5	0.6	0.8
	not at all	0.1	0.4	0.4	0.9
Denmark	very		0.3	0.6	0.7
	quite	0.3	0.4	0.4	0.6
	only a little	0.3	0.3	0.4	0.4
	not at all	0.2	0.3	0.4	0.4
France	very	1.8	1.6	1.8	1.7
	quite	0.4	1.2	1.4	1.8
	only a little	0.5	0.9	1.2	1.1
	not at all	0.6	0.7	1.3	1.5
Germany[a]	very		1.0	1.3	1.2
	quite	0.0	0.9	1.0	1.0
	only a little	0.2	0.6	0.8	0.9
	not at all	0.0	0.4	0.3	0.7
Great Britain	very	1.1	1.0	0.9	1.1
	quite	0.6	0.9	1.0	1.2
	only a little	0.4	0.6	0.7	0.7
	not at all	0.2	0.4	0.3	0.6
Ireland	very	2.2	1.5	1.8	2.1
	quite	1.4	1.2	1.4	1.9
	only a little	0.9	1.2	1.2	1.7
	not at all	0.5	1.0	1.2	1.2
Italy	very			1.5	1.4
	quite	0.0	0.8	0.4	1.2
	only a little	0.3	0.5	0.8	0.9
	not at all	0.2	0.3	0.3	0.5
Netherlands	very	0.7	1.9	2.0	2.8
	quite	0.8	1.5	2.2	2.6
	only a little	0.5	1.3	1.3	1.7
	not at all	0.5	1.1	1.4	1.9

a   In Germany, interviewers were instructed to code no more than three issues.

APPENDIX D

Discriminant function coefficients for European/domestic voting grounds (Four-variable and nine-variable analyses) (a)

Structural variables	Denmark	France	German	Great Britain	Ireland	Italy	Nether-lands
Party vote	.87	-.91	-.20	.90	-.24	.25	-.36
Sex	.16	-.32	.03	.20	-.93	.42	-.67
Age	.16	-.21	-.07	-.46	-.17	-.22	-.53
Education	.50	-.31	.97	.00	-.36	.71	-.40
Structural, opinion and campaign variables							
Party vote	-.12	-.40	.14	-.38	.22	-.15	-.07
Sex	.00	-.14	.04	-.04	.57	-.03	-.41
Age	-.03	-.15	-.03	.33	.12	.16	-.20
Education	-.32	-.18	-.39	.13	.21	-.18	-.13
Attitudes to membership	-.72	-.54	-.48	-.47	-.02	-.22	-.40
Attitudes to unification	-.22	-.21	-.17	-.19	.20	.17	-.12
Attitudes to Parliament	.16	-.27	-.07	-.20	.04	-.31	-.12
Campaign interest	.13	.02	-.47	-.17	.57	-.47	-.54
Campaign exposure	-.28	-.05	-.08	-.18	-.71	-.34	.02

a Positive coefficients represent an association with 'European' voting grounds of: male sex, older age; higher education; pro-European attitudes; higher campaign interest; and more campaign exposure. The party vote variable was created by grading the parties respondents had voted for in order corresponding to their usual supporters' attitudes to the Common Market - higher for more positive attitudes.

BIBLIOGRAPHY

Asp, Kent and Miller, Arthur H., 'Learning about Politics from the Media in Sweden and the United States', paper presented at the 1980 Annual Meeting of the American Political Science Association, Washington, August 1980.

Bibes, Genevieve, Menudier, Henri, de la Serre, Francoise and Smouts, Marie-Claude, Europe Elects Its Parliament, Policy Studies Institute, London, 1980.

Blumler, Jay G., 'Communication in the European Elections: The Case of British Broadcasting', Goverment and Opposition, Vol.14, 1979, pp.503-530.

Blumler, Jay G., 'An Overview of Recent Research into the Impact of Broadcasting in Democratic Politics', in M.J. Clark (ed), Politics and the Media: Film and Television for the Political Scientist and Historian, Pergamon Press, Oxford, 1979.

Blumler, Jay G., Cayrol, Roland and Thoveron, Gabriel, La Television Fait-Elle L'Election?, Presses de la Fondation Nationale des Sciences Politiques, Paris, 1978.

Blumler, Jay G. and Fox, Anthony, D., 'The Involvement of Voters in the European Elections of 1979: Its Extent and Sources', European Journal of Political Research, Vol.8, 1980, pp.359-385.

Blumler, Jay G. and Gurevitch, Michael, 'Towards a Comparative Framework for Political Communication Research', in Chaffee, Steven H. (ed), Political Communication: Issues and Strategies for Research, Sage, Beverly Hills and London, 1975.

Blumler, Jay G. and Gurevitch, Michael, 'Role Relationships in Political Communication', in Nimmo, D. and Sanders, K. (eds), Handbook of Political Communication, Sage, Beverly Hills, forthcoming.

Blumler, Jay G., Gurevitch, Michael and Ives, Julian, The Challenge of Election Broadcasting, Leeds University Press, Leeds, 1978.

Blumler, Jay G., McQuail, Denis and Nossiter, T.J., 'Political Communication and the Young Voter', report to the Social Science Research Council, October, 1975.

Blumler, Jay G., McQuail, Denis and Nossiter, T.J. 'Political Communication and the Young Voter in the General Election of February 1974', report to the Social Science Research Council, July, 1976.

Blumler, Jay G. and Petersen, Vibeke, 'Coordinating and Europeanising the Television Coverage: The Role of the European Broadcasting Union', paper presented to conference on 'The Role of Broadcasting in the European Parliamentary Elections of June 1979', Brussels, October, 1981.

Brants, Kees, Kok, Walther and van Praag Jnr, Philip, 'Problematic Campaigns: Political Parties and the European Elections', Intermediair, August 31st, 1979.

British Broadcasting Corporation, The Coverage of the 1974 General Election Campaign on Television and Radio, BBC, London, 1974.

British Broadcasting Corporation, The Coverage of the 1979 General Election Campaign on Television and Radio, BBC, London, 1981, Part 2.

Butler, David and Marquand, David, European Elections and British Politics, Longmans, London and New York, 1981.

Chaffee, Steven H. and Choe, Sun Yuel, 'Time of Decision and Media Use During the Ford-Carter Campaign', Public Opinion Quarterly, Vol.34, 1980, pp.53-69.

Charlot, Monica, 'Women in Politics in France', in Penniman, Howard R. (ed), The French National Assembly Elections of 1978, American Enterprise Institute for Public Policy Research, Washington, D.C., 1980.

Claeys, Paul-H and Loeb-Mayer, Nicole, 'Trans-European Party Groupings: Emergence of New and Alignment of Old Parties in the Light of the Direct Elections to the European Parliament', Government and Opposition, Vol.14, 1979.

Claeys, Paul-H, de Graeve-Lismont, Edith and Loeb-Mayer, Nicole, European or National? The 1979 Election in Belgium, Katholieke Universiteit Leuven and Universite Libre de Bruxelles, December 1980.

Collins, Neil, 'The European Direct Election Campaign in the Republic of Ireland', paper presented to Workshop on Direct Elections to the European Parliament, ECPR, Florence, March 1980.

Colombo, Emilio, Elections to the European Parliament by Direct Universal Suffrage, Directorate-General for Research and Documentation, Luxembourg, 1969.

Cotta, Maurizio, 'Italy: How a Quick Start Became a Late Arrival', in Herman, Valentine and Hagger, Mark (eds), The Legislation of Direct Elections to the European Parliament, Gower, Westmead, 1981.

Crewe, Ivor, 'Electoral Participation', in Butler, David, Penniman, Howard R. and Ranney, Austin (eds), Democracy at the Polls: A Comparative Study of Competitive National Elections, American Enterprise Institute for Public Policy Research, Washington and London, 1981.

Davis, Dennis K, 'Conceptualization of Political Culture Development: An Approach to the Analysis of the 1979 European Parliament Election', paper presented to the Midwest Association for Public Opinion Research Annual Meeting, Chicago, Illinois, December, 1980.

Dennis, J. and Chaffee, S, 'Legitimation in the 1976 Presidential Election', Communication Research, Vol.29, 1978, pp.447-468.

Feeney, Peter, 'European Elections Mark New Phase in Political Television', Irish Broadcasting Review, No.6, 1979, pp.38-42.

Feld, Werner and Wildgen, John K, 'Electoral Ambitions and European Integration', International Organisation, Vol.29, 1975, pp.447-468.

Gurevitch, Michael and Blumler, Jay G, 'Linkages Between the Mass Media and Politics: A Model for the Analysis of Political Communications Systems', in Curran, James, Gurevitch, Michael and Woollacott, Janet, (eds), Mass Communication and Society, Edward Arnold, London, 1977.

Hainsworth, Paul A, 'The European Election of 1979 in Northern Ireland: Linkage Politics', Parliamentary Affairs, Vol.32, 1979, pp.459-469.

Hedges, Alan and Courtenay, Gillian, The European Parliament: Exploratory Research, Social and Community Planning Research, London, 1978.

Herman, Valentine and Hagger, Mark, (eds), The Legislation of Direct Elections to the European Parliament, Gower, Westmead, 1981.

Herman, Valentine and Lodge, Juliet, The European Parliament and the European Community, London, Macmillan, 1978.

Herman, Valentine and Lodge, Juliet, 'Direct Elections: Outcomes and Prospects', in Herman and Hagger, (eds), op. cit., 1981.

Hollick, Julian Crandall, 'The European Election of 1979 in France: A Masked Ball for 1981', Parliamentary Affairs, Vol.32, 1979, pp.459-469.

Hoyer, S., Hadenius, S. and Weibull, L., The Politics and Economics of the Press: A Developmental Perspective, Sage, Beverly Hills and London, 1975.

Inglehart, Ronald, The Silent Revolution: Changing Values and Political Styles among Western Publics, Princeton University Press, Princeton, New Jersey, 1977.

Inglehart, Ronald, 'Long Term Trends in Mass Support for European Unification', Government and Opposition, Vol.12, 1977, pp.150-177.

Inglehart, Ronald, and Rabier, Jacques-Rene, 'Europe Elects a Parliament: Cognitive Mobilization, Political Mobilization and pro-European Attitudes as Influences on Voter Turnout', Government and Opposition, Vol.14, 1979, pp.479-507.

Inglehart, Ronald, Rabier, Jacques-Rene, Gordon, Ian and Sorensen, Carsten Lehman, 'Broader Powers for the European Parliament? The Attitudes of Candidates', European Journal of Political Research, Vol.8, 1980, pp.113-132.

Jowell, Roger and Courtenay, Gillain, European Election Study, Social and Community Planning Research, London, 1978.

Klapper, Joseph T., The Effects of Mass Communication, The Free Press of Glencoe, Illinois, 1960.

Kohn, Walter K.S.G., 'Women in the European Parliament', Parliamentary Affairs, Vol.34, 1981, pp.210-220.

Leigh, Michael, 'Linkage Politics: The French Referendum and the Paris Summit of 1972', Journal of Common Market Studies, Vol.14, 1975, pp.157-170.

Lodge, Juliet, 'The European Elections of 1979: A Problem Turnout', Parliamentary Affairs, Vol.32, No.4, 1979, pp.448-458.

Lodge, Julier, 'Germany: Modell Deutschland', in Herman and Hagger (eds), op. cit., 1981.

Lodge, Juliet and Herman, Valentine, 'Direct Elections to the European Parliament: A Supranational Perspective', European Journal of Political Research, Vol.8, 1980, pp.45-61.

Lukes, Steven, 'Political Ritual and Social Integration', Sociology, Vol.2, 1975, pp.289-308.

Marquand, David, Parliament for Europe, Jonathan Cape, London, 1979.

McOuail, Denis and Davis, Dennis, 'Preliminary Report on the Netherlands Campaign Panel Survey: European Election, 1979', unpublished report, Amsterdam, 1980.

Moxon-Browne, Edward, 'Ireland: An Eager Consummation', in Herman and Hagger (eds), op. cit., 1981.

Nixon, R. 'Freedom in the World's Press: A Fresh Appraisal with New Data', Journalism Quarterly, Vol.42, 1965, pp.3-14, 118-119.

Patijn, S. Contribution to proceedings of the European Parliament, OJ Amnex No.185, January 14, 1975.

Patterson, Thomas E, The Mass Media Election: How Americans Choose Their President, Praeger, New York, 1980.

Penniman, Howard R, 'Campaign Styles and Methods', in Butler, David, Penniman, Howard R. and Ranney, Austin, (eds), Democracy at the Polls: A Comparative Study of Competitive National Elections, American Enterprise Institute for Public Policy Research, Washington and London, 1981.

Petersen, Vibeke G. and Sauerberg, Steen, 'Danish Broadcasters and the Direct Election to the European Parliament of June 1979', paper presented to Workshop on Media and Elections, ECPR, Lancaster, March/April 1981.

Powell, G. Bingham Jnr, 'Voting Turnout in Thirty Democracies: Partisan, Legal, and Socio-Economic Influences', in Rose, Richard (ed), Electoral Participation: A Comparative Analysis, Sage, Beverly Hills and London, 1980.

Pridham, Geoffrey and Pridham, Pippa, Transnational Party Co-operation and European Integration: The Process Towards Direct Elections, George Allen and Unwin, London, 1981.

Pryce, R. 'Legitimacy and European Integration: The role of Information', paper presented to the Xth Congress of the International Political Science Association, Edinburgh, 1976.

Reif, Karlheinz and Schmitt, Hermann, 'Nine Second-Order National Elections - A conceptual Framework for the Analysis of European Election Results', European Journal of Political Research, Vol.8, 1980, pp.3-44.

Robinson, John P, 'Mass Communication and Information Diffusion', in Kline, F. Gerald and Tichenor, Phillip J. (eds), Current Perspectives in Mass Communication Research, Sage Publication Beverly Hills and London, 1972.

Sarlvik, B. and Crewe, I. Conservative Victory in Retrospect, Cambridge University Press, 1982.

Sauerberg, Steen and Thomsen, Niels, 'The Political Role of Mass Communication in Scandinavia', in Cerny, Karl H. (ed), Scandinavia at the Polls: Recent Political Trends in Denmark, Norway and Sweden, American Enterprise Institute for Public Policy Research, Washington, 1977.

Schönbach, Klaus, and Schulz, Winfried, 'Promoting a Political Symbol: The Role of the Mass Media in the First Direct Elections to the European Parliament', paper presented at XXXth International Conference on Communication of the International Communication Association, Acapulco, Mexico, 1980.

Schoul, Tove Lise, 'Denmark: The Functionalists', in Herman and Hagger (eds), op. cit., 1981.

Seymour-Ure, Colin, The Political Impact of Mass media, Constable (London) and Sage (Beverly Hills), 1974.

Shaw, Donald L. and McCombs, Maxwell E. The Emergence of American Political Issues: The Agenda-Setting Function of the Press, West Publishing Co, St. Paul, Minnesota, 1977.

Smith, Anthony (ed), Television and Political Life: Studies in Six European Countries, Macmillan, London and Basingstoke, 1979.

Star, S. and Hughes, H., 'Report on an Educational Campaign: The Cincinnati Plan for the United Nations', American Journal of Sociology, Vol.55, 1950, pp.389-400.

Steed, Michael, 'The European Parliament: The Significance of Direct Elections', Government and Opposition, Vol.6, 1971, pp.462-476.

Weaver, David H., Graber, Doris A., McCombs, Maxwell E. and Eyal, Chaim H. Media Agenda-Setting in a Presidential Election: Issues, Images, and Interest, Praeger, New York, 1981.

The POLICY STUDIES INSTITUTE (PSI) is a British independent policy research organisation concerned with issues relevant to economic and social policies and the working of political institutions.

PSI was formed in April 1978 through the merger of Political and Economic Planning (PEP), founded in 1931, and the Centre for Studies in Social Policy (CSSP), founded in 1972. It continues the tradition of both organisations to establish the facts by impartial empirical research and to relate the findings to practical policy making. The scope of the Institute's work has been extended by the recent establishment of a European Centre for Political Studies. PSI's work is financed by grants for specific studies made by trusts, foundations and public bodies, with substantial support from donations by industry and commerce, and by annual subscriptions.

The results of the studies are disseminated widely by means of frequent publications, articles and seminars.

Details of subscription rates and recent publications will be sent on request.

1-2 Castle Lane, London SW1E 6DR
Telephone: 01-828 7055

PSI publications

PSI publishes a number of REPORTS each year on topics of public interest.

In addition, full length BOOKS which incorporate the results of research projects of two or three years' duration are produced from time to time.

How to obtain PSI publications

PSI publications may be obtained from booksellers or direct from PSI. Postage and packing will be additional to the cost of the publication if it is sent by post.

PSI RECENT PUBLICATIONS

REPORTS

No.585	Japanese Industrial Policy	£3.95
No.586	Differentials for Managers and Skilled Manual Workers in the UK	£3.95
No.587	The Social Consequences of Rail Closures	£4.50
No.588	Maternity Rights: The experience of women	£4.95
No.589	Shorter Working Time	£3.95
No.590	Microprocessors in Manufactured Products	£3.25
No.591	The Economics of Historic Country Houses	£4.95
No.592	Retirement Age and Retirement Costs	£3.95
No.593	A Report from Hackney	£2.50
No.594	Unemployment and Racial Minorities	£5.00
No.595	Family Planning, Sterilisation and Abortion Services	£4.00
No.596	Maternity Rights: The experience of employers	£5.00
No.597	Case Studies of Shorter Working Time	£4.50
No.598	Policy and Practice in the Multi-Racial City	£6.50
No.599	Industrial Policy and Investment Decisions	£3.50
No.600	First Homes: A survey of the housing circumstances of young married couples	£4.50
No.601	Fuel Debts and Hardship	£5.00
No.602	Family Care of the Handicapped Elderly: Who Pays?	£3.50
No.603	Microelectronics in Industry: What's Happening in Britain	£5.00

DISCUSSION PAPERS

No. 1	Discussing the Welfare State	£2.75
No. 2	Diversity and Decentralisation in the Welfare State	£2.75
No. 3	Public Policy and Family Life	£2.75
No. 4	A New Look at the Personal Social Services	£3.75
No. 5	Wilson Revisited: Industrialists and Financiers	£2.50

STUDIES IN EUROPEAN POLITICS

1.	The Future of the European Parliament	£3.95
2.	Towards Transnational Parties in the European Community	£1.80
3.	European Integration, Regional Devolution and National Parliaments	£2.25
4.	Eurocommunism and Foreign Policy	£2.95
5.	Europe Elects its Parliament	£3.50

BOOKS

Overseas Doctors in the National Health Service
David J. Smith £12.00

Governments and Trade Unions
Denis Barnes and Eileen Reid .... £12.50 (Cased)
£6.50 (Paper)

Rational Techniques in Policy Analysis
Michael Carley .... £12.50 (Cased)
£5.50 (Paper)

Parliaments and Economic Affairs
David Coombes and S.A. Walkland (eds.) £13.00

Women in Top Jobs
Michael Fogarty, Isobel Allen and Patricia Walters £14.00

Evaluative Research in Social Care
E. Matilda Goldberg and Naomi Connelly (eds.) .... £15.00 (Cased)
£7.50 (Paper)

Fifty Years of Political and Economic Planning
Poverty and the Development of Anti-Poverty Policy
in the UK
Richard Berthoud and Joan C. Brown .... £13.50 (Cased)
£6.50 (Paper)

Representative Government and Economic Power
David Coombes .... £15.00 (Cased)
£6.95 (Paper)

RESEARCH PAPERS

Social Impact Assessment: A Cross Disciplinary Guide to the Literature	£3.50
Social Security and Welfare Benefit Schemes	£2.50
The Unemployed Flow	£7.50
Microprocessor Short Courses	£5.00
Microelectronics in Industry: Extent of Use	£5.00
Social Services Provision in Multi-Racial Areas	£3.75
Ethnic Record Keeping in Local Authorities	£1.50
Microelectronics in Industry: Advantages and Problems	£5.00
Microelectronics in Industry: Awareness and Government Support	£5.00
Microelectronics in Industry: Manpower and Training	£5.00
Ageing, Needs and Nutrition	£5.00
Postgraduate Education in Universities and Polytechnics	£6.00
The Employment of Postgraduates	£6.00